Tricked Out Toolbox
Promotion and Marketing Tools Every Writer Needs

What's in your toolbox?

By Tonya Kappes and Melissa Bourbon Ramirez

The Tricked Out Toolbox
Copyright 2012 Melissa Ramirez Bourbon and Tonya
Kappes
PrintISBN-13:978-1469962870
ISBN-10:146996287X

Cover Art Design by A.J. Ramirez

*Graphic images (toolbox, hammer, keyboard) licensed by
istockphoto.com and bigstockphoto.com*

*The authors warrant that all quotes from industry
professionals are used with permission and that the
proper documentation is on file with the publisher.*

The book is dedicated to writers everywhere, introverts and extroverts alike.

~Melissa and Tonya

Whether you're just sticking your toe into the murky waters of the publishing industry, traversing the white waters of your already established career, or somewhere in between, The Tricked Out Toolbox is for you.

In The Tricked Out Toolbox, you'll identify your personality type: introvert or extrovert. Read anecdotes from authors about what's worked for them and what hasn't. Get ideas, craft a budget, build a marketing plan, and learn how to execute it.

With checklists and worksheets galore, real-life advice, and an easy to read format, this user-friendly, practical guide allows you to pick and chose what promotion and marketing tools will work for you. If you buy one business book this year, make it The Tricked Out Toolbox.

"In today's tough market, savvy promotion is often a key ingredient to an author's success, but few authors are familiar with all the tools available to them. They spend a fortune on the things that don't work and overlook opportunities that might create more impact. That's why I'm thrilled Melissa Bourbon and Tonya Kappes have taken on this aspect of the writer's life and demystified the process. In Tricked Out Toolbox, the new author has all she needs to successfully promote her latest book." ~ Brenda Novak

Helpful symbols used throughout the book:

 Moments in the book when Tonya or Melissa gives an example by telling a personal story.

 Sprinkled throughout are quotes by authors, industry professionals, and readers.

 Essential tools for your promotional/marketing toolbox.

 Notable information

Table of Contents

Introduction

Let's be crystal clear. You're only as good as your next book and the best marketing and promotion money can buy won't guarantee sales. People have to connect to your books each and every time they pick a new one up.

That being said, we're here to tell you that writing a great book isn't enough. You can spend $15,000 to market and promote your book and have lackluster sales; or you can spend $1,000 and hit best seller list after list after list. Bottom line? There's no silver bullet. It's up to you to do what you can to build your career. In the day and age of e-books, independent digital publishers, brick and mortar stores closing left and right, and the changing face of publishing, marketing and promotion have never been more important. Getting your book in front of readers is paramount, but how do you do that?

First, identify your personality strengths. An author who is an extrovert will do well at book signings, talking to booksellers, and interacting with readers face to face. An introvert will do better focusing on online promotion. Finding balance, knowing your options and coming up with a plan will give you an edge toward success.

Our journeys began at different times, and under different circumstances. We showed up on blogs, at conferences . . .everywhere—and we mean everywhere—as we learned about the publishing business. We ended up blog friends, and then together we created The Naked Hero. We put ourselves out there, positioning our grog on the Internet, talking it up at workshops, conferences, and local meetings. We were in everyone's face about The Naked Hero.

The buzz had begun. Opportunity was knocking…and we answered the door!

Before long, we began to hear comments about how great we were at promoting our website. We started from scratch, with nothing more than a nugget of an idea, and now our traffic and site statistics are off the charts. We've been promotion and marketing students, and now we're teachers, sharing what we've learned.

When we started The Naked Hero, Tonya didn't have a book to promote, but she knew she was going to garner a lot of positive exposure for when she began to self publish. Melissa had *Living the Vida Lola, a Lola Cruz Mystery* under her belt. *Hasta La Vista Lola* was coming out and she was actively building her online platform.

There are scads of books out there on marketing and promotion. What makes this book different is the practical, tried-and-true approach we've taken. We've walked the walk, talked the talk, and now we're sharing what we've learned with you. Why reinvent the wheel when you don't have to? We've done the legwork for you. So get your toolbox out, load up that Bedazzler, and get ready to polish the tools you need to maximize your marketing and publicity efforts so you can stick to what it is you love doing: writing.

We know that all writers are as different as their books. We understand each other and can talk endlessly about writing and the industry, but we've found that writing and PR/marketing are like oil and vinegar. We live in our heads, with our characters, so putting ourselves out there to talk up our own work is tough. We grew up with our parents telling us not to brag or boast. But writing and finishing a novel is not an easy feat! So we say brag! No one else is going to do it for you.

The *Tricked Out Toolbox* will arm you with the best promotional and marketing tools to put in your toolbox, no matter what personality type you are.

So strap on that tool belt, lace up those boots (or slip on those high-heels), grab your hard hat or your feather boa, and get ready to stuff your toolbox.

Section One: Designing Your Blueprints

When builders begin to build a house, they start with sketches, a design, blueprints, and building plans. They know what they want the house to look like. They visit hardware stores to order the materials on their list. They grab their toolboxes and any equipment they'll need. They work with subcontractors. And with some hard work, craftsmanship, and know-how, they bring the house they envisioned to life.

The same holds true for writers. We start with an idea, develop characters, and begin to plot. Whether you're a pantser, like Tonya, a plotter, like so many writers, or somewhere in between, like Melissa, we all start with a nugget of an idea. Eventually these ideas start to take the shape of a book and we are off and running.

That's the creative side of doing what we love. We create worlds out of thin air, worlds so real that we can't wait to sit down at our computers and put fingers to keyboards. But what do you do when you're done typing, the story is finished, and you're working on selling the book? How are you going to tell people about it? How can you make your book stand out in this crazy competitive publishing market?

You're reading The *Tricked Out Toolbox*, so you're on the right track. We'll take you through marketing and promotion, step by step. From figuring out who your target audience is to building a website, you'll come away with the tools you need to build a successful writing career.

Use the appendices in the back of this book to help you identify your goals, dreams you dare to dream, the steps of your action plan, a workable budget, and your timeframe.

Chapter One: Understanding your Marketing and Promotion Personality

In this chapter:
- Understanding your PR personality
- Personality Quiz

Understanding Your PR Personality
Just like builders, every writer has their own marketing style. Red brick or siding? Hardwood floors or tile? Stainless steel or utilitarian? We have similar decisions to make. Website or blog? Publicist or no? Big budget or PR (public relations) on a dime?

Decisions, decisions, decisions.

You have to know yourself before you can know how to market yourself. YES! We said it…er…typed it. The key word is yourself. It's up to you to get word of your novel outside the realm of your family and friends.

Figuring out your marketing and promotional personality is a very important tool for your toolbox.

You need to know what marketing and promotion personality you have before you can start developing your plans. Why? Because your personality will drive the direction of your marketing and promotion efforts. It's all about knowing your strengths and weaknesses…and working toward the former.

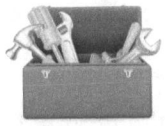 **Toolbox Essential**:

Figuring out what your strengths are may take time now, but it'll save you time later.

Are you shy? You might write articles to put in your toolbox. Are you super outgoing and schmoozing is your specialty? You might put volunteering in your toolbox.

Personality Quiz

Take this quick quiz to identify your personality strengths.

1. Do you consider yourself a people person with a lot of friends?
   a. ❑ Totally. The better question would be...who ISN'T my friend?
   b. ❑ Not really. I have a few friends, but I usually only talk to them one at a time.
2. Do you consider yourself an...
   a. ❑ extrovert.
   b. ❑ introvert.

3. What room in your house do you like to spend more time?
   a. ❏ I love spending time in my bedroom because it's my space and it's quiet.
   b. ❏ In the living room, of course, because that's where the action is.
4. Are you loud or quiet?
   a. ❏ Totally loud, baby!
   b. ❏ Definitely more quiet.
5. You've had a long day. To wind down, you prefer to:
   a. ❏ hang around at home, listen to music, and just have quiet time.
   b. ❏ get my peeps and hit the town.
6. How does the idea of talking to readers at a book signing make you feel?
   a. ❏ Scared out of my mind.
   b. ❏ Excited! Can't wait to get around all those people.
7. There's a conference coming up and they need speakers. What do you do?
   a. ❏ Dodge the incoming phone calls from the conference coordinator.
   b. ❏ Jump at the chance. Who cares if I have nothing to say? I can bluff my way through.
8. In school, there were collaborative learning groups. How did you feel about them?
   a. ❏ I would much rather work on my own.
   b. ❏ Groups are AWESOME!

9. Your local writing chapter has board positions to fill. What do you do?
   a. ❏ Decline the offer. I don't like speaking in front of groups.
   b. ❏ Jump in and volunteer to be president.
10. If you're invited to join a critique group, what do you say?
    a. ❏ "I'd rather just critique one on one."
    b. ❏ "I'd love to. How many pages can I bring?"

So how'd you score?

More As than Bs? You're in introvert.
More Bs than As? Extrovert alert!

File this away as you pick tools to stuff in your toolbox. You don't want to set yourself up for failure by choosing tools you won't be comfortable using.

 **Toolbox Essetal:**

Determining your PR personality is important for your marketing and promotion future. It's crucial to know yourself and play to your strengths to increase the effectiveness of your marketing plan.

Chapter Two: It's Never Too Early to Start Marketing Yourself

In this chapter:
- Identifying your target audience: WHO are your potential readers?
- Identifying your goals
- Having an action plan
- Creating a timeline
- Developing a budget

"But I haven't even finished my book!" Is this what you're thinking?

STOP! We're here to tell you, it's NEVER too early to start marketing yourself. Just how do you do that?

Simple. Start With a Killer Marketing Plan.

Sometimes you have to start at the end and work your way forward. All the time you've been writing and dreaming of the day you see your name in print, did you ever think about the business side of publishing?

We are willing to bet that most of you didn't. We can hear your words echoing in our ears.

"Writing is creative!"

"Writing is my passion!"

"Let the publisher handle the marketing and promotion!"

No, no, no.

If this is your attitude, you are way off-base. First and foremost, we want you to understand that publishing is a business.

B.U.S.I.N.E.S.S.

And we're about to pull the rug out from under you. Here it is. Wait for it....

Getting "the call" is not the end goal.

Getting "the call" truly is JUST THE BEGINNING.

> "I think the biggest mistake on promo is not to get it out soon enough. You need to start the buzz with promo mailings, online contests, teasers, banners, blogs, Facebook etc."
> ~Dianne Castell, author, www.diannecastell.com

Are you scratching your head, wondering just what can possibly come post call? After all, you've written the book. You've landed the agent, and the agent sold your manuscript. Now you have the editor and they'll champion your book in their publishing house until the release date. Or you sold it straight to the publisher. Or self published. Whatever publishing road your book is on, you still have to promote yourself and the earlier the better.

And after that? Well, your book will be a juggernaut and it'll land on the NY Times Best Seller list, the USA Today list, and the awards will be piling in.

Won't they?

The truth is that while you may have written the best book in the history of fiction, and your editor will shout it from the rooftop as often and as loud as she can, it's a long, hard, hilly road to success. The terrain is filled with obstacles: namely the other 275,232 some odd books that will be published this year. How in the world is your book going to get noticed?

Marketing and promotion, that's how.

Before we really dig in, let's brush up on some basic book publishing statistics (bowker.com):

- 57% of book buyers are women, yet women purchase 65% of the books sold in the U.S.
- Mystery books are the most popular genre for book club sales, with 17% of all purchases of mystery books coming directly from book clubs.
- Generation X consumers buy more books online than any other demographic group, with 30% of them buying their books via the Internet.
- 21% of book buyers said they became aware of a book through some sort of online promotion or ad.
- Women make the majority of the purchases in the paperback, hardcover and audio-book segments, but men account for 55% of e-book purchases.

Information is knowledge. But now what? Let's start with the question: how do we target those book readers, whether they lean toward print or digital versions, and get them to plunk down their money for our books?

Start with a Killer Marketing Plan. (See Appendix A)

Any marketing plan needs certain key and essential components. They include:

- Identifying your target audience: WHO are your potential readers?
- Identifying your goals
- Having an action plan
- Creating a timeline
- Developing a budget
- Creating a brand

Your marketing plan is also fluid. Ideally, you are continuing to write that next novel and you don't have valuable time to waste on a plan that's not working. Developing a marketing plan, which you continually revise and refine, will help you quickly recognize what works for you, what doesn't, and how to spend your precious time, money, and energy.

Building Your Action Plan

(See Appendix A: Killer Marketing Plan; Appendix B: Action Plan Checklist; Appendix C: Laying Out Your Action Plan Timeframe)

Let's take each of the marketing plan's components and break them down. First up is identifying your audience.

Targeting Your Audience

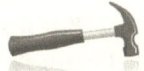

Melissa's target audiences:

- Women mystery readers
- Lovers of Charlaine Harris's mystery series, Sue Grafton, the Stephanie Plum series, and the like
- Latinas (since Lola Cruz is a Mexican-American private investigator)
- Women romance readers (since the Lola Cruz series is a hybrid: part mystery/part romance)
- Cozy mystery lovers
- Seamstresses/crafty women

Tonya's target audiences:

- Women mystery readers
- Lovers of Nancy Drew, Janet Evanovich, Heather Webber, and other cozy mystery writers.
- Anyone who loves to read about quirky characters.
- Women's fiction readers
- Chick-lit readers

Hopefully as you were writing your book, you had a general idea of who you were writing for. Are you targeting the YA market? Historical? Romance readers? Are you hoping to break out and cross genres with a mass market thriller? Knowing this as you are creating your marketing plan (and putting it into action) is just as important as knowing it as you write. Once you know who your potential readers are, you can figure out how to market directly to them.

Make a list of your perfect readers. Are they men? Women? Teens or adults? What similar authors or books do they read? Make your list as detailed as possible.

Goal Setting

Goals are the desired results you seek. In a marketing plan, they are the overarching or broad statements that will drive the elements of your plan and the steps you will take as you put your plan into action.

What are your goals as a writer?

Do you want to be a NY Times bestseller? Want to be on the USA Today list? Or are your goals more modest? Maybe you just want to earn through your first advance and have your publisher pick up your option. Or maybe you have no dreams of bestsellerdom or money in the bank. Maybe your motivation to write is the simple fact that you have a story to tell and share.

Whatever goals you have must be defined. Put them into words. Once you know what your true goals are, you have something concrete to work toward. You are focused. If the best seller list is your ultimate goal, then you will have to work hard to get there. No work, no reward. (See Appendix D: Goal Setting (Dare to Dream)

Many people believe in the power of intention. Vision boards are a great (and fun) way to identify your goals and set your intentions. Look at www.oprah.com (O Dream Board) or www.tut.com for online vision board building or get creative with tagboard, magazines, and glue.

Action Plan

Identifying your goals gives you a solid foundation, but what will it take to reach them? That's what your action plan is all about.

An action plan is the breakdown of the concrete elements you intend to act on as you market yourself and promote your book. Writing your action plan will take some time and thought. Don't rush through it, and remember, it's fluid! (See Appendix A: Killer Marketing Plan and Appendix C: Laying Out Your Action Plan)

You must take specific steps. Imagine you are a teacher and you have to teach your students to write a five sentence paragraph. Do you pass out a sheet of paper and tell them to write, stand back, and watch the brilliance flow from graphite to paper?

Ha! No way! You have to break it down for your students, one step at a time. First you teach the topic sentence. Then you teach supporting and detail sentences. Finally, you teach the concluding sentence.

It's the same with your marketing plan. You have a goal: to sell enough books to earn through your advance (or become a NY Times Best Seller). Whatever you DARED TO DREAM: (Appendix D). Now you outline the steps that will lead you to your goal.

You may want to use some or all of the following to reach your goals:

- Set up a blog tour to gain exposure.
- Set up local signings.
- Blog with intention: this is key! You have to have a platform and reason why people want to keep coming back.
- Solicit reviews at online review sites.
- Create printable promotion tools.
- Do targeted mailings of postcards and/or bookmarks.
- Set up radio interviews.

These steps are all part of your action plan, but you can't leave it at this. Some of these steps are too abstract, or require further dissection. Think back to the teacher who has to get her students to write a paragraph. Just like she broke her lesson into mini-lessons, you must break your larger steps into smaller steps.

Let's look more closely at setting up radio interviews. Set up a micro action plan for that goal.

Setting up Radio Interviews
- Create a press kit (see Appendix E)
- Identify potential radio venues and Public Relations (PR) managers
- Send out your press kit to radio stations' PR managers
- Send out press releases about your book (see Appendix L)
- Follow up with phone calls (this is key, don't be afraid of the telephone! It is your friend.)
- Try to set up one interview a week (or one a month—whatever you feel is attainable).

The micro-action plan allows you to identify the steps necessary to realize the correlating goal. As a result, the tasks before you become less daunting.

The bottom line is that you needn't be afraid to have high expectations. When we reach for the stars, we have the potential of touching one. If we don't even try, we've sealed our fate before we ever started. Small steps make up your bigger plan. Together, the pieces create a plan that will gain exposure for your book and help you reach your Dare to Dream goals.

Timeline
What is your timeframe for your Marketing Plan? (See Appendix C: Laying Out Your Action Plan Timeframe) Working within a finite period of time (four

months, or six months, for example), makes your plan manageable. It also creates deadlines for you to work toward, and we all know writers love deadlines!

You may want to start with a short timeframe for your marketing/promotion endeavors (three to six months), but as you become more comfortable with marketing and promotion, you can expand to a six to twelve month plan.

Marketing and publicity build over time. Understand that most people don't have overnight success. Be realistic about your timeframe for reaching your goals. Pace yourself and allow plenty of lead time as your release day approaches. Again, laying the foundation before you are even published is a smart move.

For example:

- 5 months prior to your release, create bookmarks and the like
- 4 months prior, target independent booksellers to send your mailing
- 4 months prior, create your press kit and identify who you will send them to
- 3 months prior, send out your press kits
- 3 months prior, set up blog tours, guest blog spots, and other online opportunities
- 2 months prior, contact local booksellers and set up signings, a release party, etc
- 1 month prior, look for loose ends and fill in the gaps!

""

""

A sample outline would look something like this:

"Six months out:

- get contacts for guest blogs, interviews etc.
- put ad on Romance Sells
- update your Facebook page, website, etc.

Three months out:

- Pat Rouse's list mailings*
- RT mailers, flyers, and bookmarks
- RT includes your flyers, postcards, and bookmarks to 700 romance friendly bookstores

One month out:

- Banners at romance websites to start buzz
- Your Facebook contests, website contests, etc.

*Pat Rouse's list is list of romance/mystery/fantasy bookstores and reader's groups. You buy the updated list at RousePat@aol.com"

~Duffy Brown, Iced Chiffon, Berkley Prime Crime

Budgeting

What about Budget? (See Appendix F) "Show me the money!" Jerry Maguire famously says.

Most of us don't make a ton of money on our first (or subsequent) advance. If you have a marketing budget that allows you the freedom to spend and market widely, you are in a great position—and the rest of us are completely jealous.

If your budget is limited, like the majority of us, plan accordingly. Look for free publicity/marketing opportunities. Don't pay someone else to set up a blog tour; set it up yourself. Contact the people behind your favorite blogs and line up guest spots. Make your contact personal, though. As co-founders of The Naked Hero, we get authors wanting to post guest hero profiles. We LOVE our guests. But what we don't love are the mass emails that come through occasionally from someone who doesn't know what The Naked Hero is about, or hasn't looked into the type of columns we post. That doesn't help us feel the love.

Make the bloggers you contact feel a connection with you. It's key, and it's good karma. The writing community is one of the most supportive groups of people out there; be part of it.

Some potential expenditures you should consider and factor into your budget are:

- Postage for mailing ARCs to reviewers and/or contest winners
- Postcards, bookmarks, other marketing materials
- Paying for advertising or exposure [such as at Books on the House (booksonthehouse.com), a fantastic opportunity for all authors], banners, Kindle Nation Daily Pushes, EReader New Today, etc...
- Development of a website and/or blog site (hosting fees, domain name, design fees)
- Press Release materials

Chapter Three: What Brand is in Your Toolbox?

In this Chapter:
- What is a brand
- How to discover your brand
- Why knowing your brand is important
- The importance of a tagline

What is Branding?

66
99 "Personal branding simply stated: your Personal Brand is what others think of when they think of you (and your work). It's a simple set of phrases, images and impressions that help form a definition of a given person (or organization)." Branding expert, Jenn Stark, Jennstark.com.

Ask five people what branding is and you'll get five similar answers. People understand the basic concept of branding. When a customer hears your name or picks up a product, they have an immediate and strong impression of what they're going to get. Read a John Grisham book and you're in for a legal thriller with a smidgeon of romance. Pick up a Lola Cruz Mystery and you'll get a smart and sassy PI read with enough family drama to make it interesting and enough spice to give a little thrill and anticipation.

Let's be clear, branding is NOT about a tagline; branding is about reader expectation. That's not to say that a tagline isn't important, but ultimately, branding is about what a reader is going to experience while reading your books. Author Angi Morgan says it's like buying Campbell's Soup or Pepsi. You know you can count on the product living up to your expectation.

Put another way, branding is your image within the writing world. It frames how other writers, readers, booksellers, librarians, agents, and editors see you.

You write because you love it…yeah, we've said it and we meant it, but we're talking business now. Building a brand is another way to help readers find you.

One question people have is whether or not branding limits a writer's options or pigeonholes them, slotting them into one genre and limiting their range and/or options. We don't believe so. Think of Jayne Ann Krentz, aka Amanda Quick, aka Jayne Castle. One writer, three personas. Same basic style of writing, pacing, and voice, but one series is contemporary, one is paranormal, and one is historical. The pen name tells the reader which type of book they're getting; the brand tells them what the voice and style will be and what to expect from the read. The reader will always know what they're going to get when they pick up a book by an author who has effectively branded him or herself.

The long and short of it is that branding is the heart of your writing image.

 Aspiring women's fiction writer Tracy Ward says branding is about name recognition. "When I pick up a Nora

Roberts book, I know what it is and what it'll be: Contemporary with a paranormal spin and, more than likely, part of a trilogy, because that's what she writes. Janet Evanovich's brand is Stephanie Plum. Anything by Mariann Keys will be about an Irish girl in the city."

The end goal is to have your name become your brand. The tagline acts as a bridge between your name and your book. Nora Roberts' brand, like John Grisham, JK Rowling, James Patterson, and Jodi Picoult, has become brand synonymous with her name. Name recognition is all it takes for a reader to buy a Nora Roberts or a James Patterson book.

Discovering Your Brand
Developing your brand can be broken up into three separate stages. (See Appendix G)

If you write nonfiction, you probably are your brand. Nonfiction authors build their brand based on their platform and credentials. Margie Lawson has built her brand on Empowering Character Emotion through Deep Edits. Deb Dixon built hers on Goal, Motivation, and Conflict. Their credentials come from their success as fiction writers, but their nonfiction platform sells itself.

Step 1: Your Story is Important.

Readers love to hear about you, your road to publishing, and what your life is like. It gives them an emotional connection with you. It allows them to see you are human just like them.

"I wrote my first novel under the tree during my son's football practice and in the car while waiting for my boys in car line. That is the truth. When I tell readers this, they see that I'm a working mom, just like them. It opens up a door to conversation about family. Now we have something in common and we are tied together. That reader will remember me." ~Tonya

Knowing who you are, so that your media image matches the brand you create, is important. Are you sophisticated, like Brenda Novak, and does your image match that tagline? Or are you a country girl, like Tonya, your stories and image blending together to create a complete picture? Or maybe you're "Latina-by-marriage", like Melissa's alter-ego, Misa Ramirez, blending two cultures together through your stories.

Step Two: Perception and Voice

We are here to lay it all out there for you, right or wrong, good or bad. We're telling you like it is. That being said, everyone knows the saying, "Perception is everything." Take it to heart because it is the truth.

Unfortunately, people judge each other by first impressions. It's just like a book cover. A reader will look at a front book cover for less than 8 seconds, flip it over and look at the back for about 15 seconds, read the first sentence—maybe—then decide if they are going to plunk down the money to buy it.

We promise you, side by side, authors' names covered, if we put an ugly book cover next to a gorgeous one, you'll pick the gorgeous cover every time. This principle applies to websites and blogs, as well.

 **Toolbox Essential:**

If you're an extrovert, make sure you talk to every author and every reader you can connect with. If you are at a book signing supporting some of your author friends, introduce yourself to the bookseller. Let the writing community see that you are approachable.

Unfortunately, the same is true behind the scenes. Studies show that a less attractive, confident person attracts attention more than an unconfident, pretty person. So always do your best to appear pulled together, act professional, and exude confidence. This includes your behavior, participation, and attitude on your website, blogs, social networks. It also applies when visiting other people's websites and blogs.

Get a professional picture taken for your author photo. Choose pictures for your Facebook profile that blend with your writer persona. But most of all, radiate confidence! You'll attract the attention you want and the readers you need.

People will always be looking at how you carry yourself at book signings, conferences, workshops, or wherever else you represent yourself as a writer. It's important to your brand to always try to look your best and appear professional. Live up to people's perception of you.

So what does it mean have a persona that blends with who you are as a writer? It comes down to thinking about how you do (or will) portray yourself to the public. Keep in mind your PR personality we discussed in Chapter One to help you.

To get you thinking about it, we've provided a list of characteristics for you to peruse. Which do you identify with? Pick as many as you feel are applicable to you.

- ❏ Sophisticated
- ❏ Suburban
- ❏ Sexy
- ❏ Erotic
- ❏ Nurturing
- ❏ Responsible
- ❏ Pop-culture
- ❏ Buttoned-Up
- ❏ Fun
- ❏ Smart
- ❏ Zany
- ❏ Silly
- ❏ Dark
- ❏ Mysterious
- ❏ Intellectual
- ❏ Bad Boy

- ❏ Country
- ❏ Urban
- ❏ Girl or Boy-Next-Door
- ❏ Matronly
- ❏ Charming
- ❏ Liberated
- ❏ Political
- ❏ Wacky
- ❏ Sassy
- ❏ Flirtatious
- ❏ Best Friend
- ❏ Serious
- ❏ Spooky
- ❏ Studly
- ❏ Professor-like
- ❏ Warrior

Think about the characteristics you selected. Does your media image match or blend with any of them? Now whittle the list down to the two or three you feel you identify with MOST, and which also blend with your image or how you feel people perceive you. If necessary, think about how you can shift your media image to more closely match how you perceive yourself.

Sherrilyn Kenyon writes historical under the name Kinley MacGregor, but when she does book signings as Sherrilyn Kenyon, she often dresses the part, living up to reader expectation of her brand, blending her paranormal voice with her look.

Perception and voice go hand in hand. Voice comes from theme, tone (diction, imagery, syntax), and your perspective on life. It is unique unto you. No one has a voice like you.

Tonya's voice is humorous, witty, and caring, all wrapped up into one. Her readers laugh and cry all from the same book. Melissa's voice, on the other hand, centers around family, culture, smart women, and murder.

Knowing your voice helps you further define your brand.

Toolbox Essentials:

A brand is one of the most important tools to put in your toolbox. Use it to create a tagline, and then use your tagline on your website and promo materials.

Brand is also reflected visually (on your blog, website, and promo materials, for example):

- Sophisticated and evocative = warm colors and tones

- Quirky and fun = bright colors

You get the idea.

"When I was deciding on a tagline, I wanted to incorporate my quirky, humorous style of writing and my own personal image. When you first meet me, you'll find I love nice things and I have a strong country accent—not southern, two very different things. I can talk to anyone about anything. I wanted to be approachable. I want people to tell me my tagline makes them laugh and think 'I'm going to read her books and

feel good afterward.' That is a dream come true for me."
~Tonya

Stage Three: Creating your Tagline

Having a tagline will help cement your brand image.
Go back to that checklist of characteristics. Think about
the image you want to portray to the world, the themes
you gravitate toward with your reading selections and
your own writing, and other elements of your voice.

Take these elements and blend them together,
finessing them into a tagline that represents your writing.

"Smart and spicy mysteries." Melissa's tagline for
her Lola Cruz Mysteries reflects the essence of the series.
Once you know she writes mysteries, your immediate
response is that the books will be fun, and a little sexy.
"Dressmaking, Magic, and Mystery: the Cozy Way" is
the tagline for Melissa Ramirez's A Magical
Dressmaking Mystery Series with NAL. You
immediately get a sense that the series is kind of like
Project Runway meets Bewitched, with a murder thrown
in.

Tonya's tagline, "Quirky Creations from a High-
class Hillbilly", makes you laugh. High-class
hillbilly—what *is* that?

Can you imagine the disappointment if you met
Tonya and she was this shy writer with a New York City
accent? We think you'd feel pretty deceived. Tonya
would lose face with her readers and the trust level would
be gone. She'd have to go through a re-branding change
in order to gain her readers' trust again. Re-branding is
pretty hard to do, so do it right this first time.

Toolbox Essential:

Start playing around with different words to come up with a tagline. Try to incorporate your personality into it. (see Appendix H)

A tagline helps the reader make a connection between the book and what emotions they'll experience while reading it. Romantic suspense author Brenda Novak's tagline reads "Sophisticated, evocative romantic suspense."

Based on the tagline, you know what you're going to get: a book about sophisticated characters experiencing a little bit of romantic excitement and a whole lot of suspense. When you look and talk to Brenda, you will find she's a very sophisticated and well-spoken writer. Read her books, and you experience evocative sophistication. Brenda Novak's tagline embodies her brand.

You've got your story, your image, your voice, and your tagline.

So what now? It's time to put that brand out there for people to see.

Toolbox Essential:

Research shows that it takes seeing something 7 to 10 times before it becomes something familiar, and over 25 times for it to be recalled.

Remember, a brand is a product in a market. Think about chocolate...okay, focus here! There are so many types of chocolate to choose from. You might like milk chocolate, but your friend might like dark chocolate. Not everyone has the same taste.

You want to reach the people who like what you write. Your tagline and the brand you create will help you find those readers. Represent your brand on your website, pre-published business cards, blog comments, social networks, interviews or anywhere you may be. It's important for people to see your name over and over for them to remember you. Seeing a tagline will help readers connect with what you write.

Your brand is as strong as your voice. Embrace it and make the best impression you can the first time out of the gate!

Chapter Four: The 411 on Websites

In this chapter:
- Moving Forward: Starting at the End
- Building an Effective Website
- Website Platform

We're sure you've all heard that head-scratching riddle: What came first, the chicken or the egg? Here's a writer's version: What comes first, the author or the website?

If you are serious about your writing career, you know the answer to this riddle isn't quite as abstract as the chicken and the egg conundrum. You're a writer, first and foremost. But if you've finished a manuscript and you're moving ahead on the writer's path, then it's time to start acting like a professional writer. And that means it's time to think about the website (or think about reinventing the one you already have).

Here's the bottom line: Creating a web presence in the writing community is important. Agent Holly Root, of Waxman Literary Agency (waxmanagency.com), believes that websites help her get a sense of who the authors she's interested in are as people. But here's the thing, the presence you're creating has to be memorable—in a good way. It has to have purpose, meaning, and be well-executed. It has to be done with flair, personality, but above all, it must be done well.

Moving Forward: Starting at the End

AuthorBuzz founder, MJ Rose, believes you can spend way too much money on a website and that it should be a minimal part of your overall marketing budget. "Yes," she says, "you need a website, but it doesn't need to be complicated. People go to your website after they hear about you or your book. No one wakes up and says I'm going to start searching for websites of authors I never heard of."

So, you've decided it's time to put together that author website you've been thinking about, but where do you start? Most people would say, "Start at the beginning." We're going to tell you the opposite.

That's right. Start at the end.

Just like mystery writers generally begin a book by knowing just how a crime was committed, and whodunit, you need to know what your end goal is with your website.

Ask yourself this question:

Just what do you hope to accomplish and project with your website?

Like that mystery writer, work backwards.

Building an Effective Website

Step One:

Know your end goal. Determining your purpose—meaning what you want people to take away from your site—is key.

Once you've figured that out, you can fill in the content with ease.

Let's go through the process of determining just what your website should accomplish.

You're an author. You're submitting your work to agents, and maybe to editors, all in the hopes of getting an offer of representation or publication. The potential agent/editor likes your voice and thinks your writing has potential. They see you have a website and immediately think, "Great, she has a jump on the marketing/promotion angle." Anything that will help sales and gain exposure for an author is a good thing, right?

NO! In Holly Root's opinion, an outdated look, outdated information, and a site that is too personal, and consequently unprofessional, is a detriment. "I've never said no because of a bad site, but it doesn't make me eager to say yes."

Again, start with the end in mind. You want your website to:

- Have a professional look
- Capture the flavor and/or voice of your book

- Be crisp and easy to navigate
- Have relevant and fresh content
- If it includes a blog, be sure the blog offers something unique in cyberspace and that you don't write things you may regret at some future date

> " NYT bestselling author Brenda Novak (brendanovak.com) has this advice: "A website is important for anyone who's really serious about becoming a professional writer. Just as you lay the foundation for selling your first book by finishing a manuscript and submitting, you lay the foundation for the promotion side of your business by creating a great website, one where you can begin to establish a presence in the community."

Always keep in mind that you are selling yourself as an author.

Agents and editors don't care what you do in your spare time, how much coffee you drink at Starbies, how much sleep you got last night, or who you partied with.

When you're published, your readers might want to know some of this, but remember to keep your goal in mind; be professional. You never know whose looking. Toni Plummer, editor at Thomas Dunne Books, an imprint of St. Martin's Press, says that if you haven't yet sold a book, a website isn't absolutely essential, but it can't hurt. "Posting part of the manuscript may get some attention. *But the pages have to be good!* Really good. This is especially beneficial if you have contacts with authors, preferably well-known and respected ones, who can comment on your work. Some writers have managed to get a book deal this way."

Step Two:

You have your end goal in mind; you're a professional writer and you're presenting yourself to the writing community at large.

Now let's take a closer look at the most important elements of a website:

- Creating a brand (see Chapter Three).
- Simplicity. A website must be easy to navigate. Make it crystal clear what type of book you're promoting. Brenda Novak says, "No one has the patience to hunt for information they expect to be at their fingertips."
- Fresh Content
- The front page of your website creates a first impression. Does it tell readers what you are about and what they can expect from your books? Are the colors, tone, language, graphics, and overall visuals in line with your style of writing? They should be.
- Your website should reflect the tone of your book. It should have the same voice. Your book, your website, your brand, and your tagline are all parts of the same puzzle. They must complement each other.

Take a few minutes to look at these other author sites: Laura Weisberger (www.laurenweisberger.com), Lisa Kleypas (www.lisakleypas.com), and Allison Brennan (www.allisonbrennan.com).

They are all miles apart from each other with branding, tone, color, and style, but they all have one thing in common. They have structural simplicity with ease of navigation. They are not cluttered. They do not overwhelm. They flow, neatly direct visitors to wherever they want to go, and they are easy on the eye.

 "When in doubt," Holly Root says, "go simple. Animated gifs are not your friend."

You want people to visit and revisit your website. In order for those return visits to happen, there must be fresh, meaningful content. That means your website is a time investment. It's another thing that you must manage. You need to be changing and adding content constantly in order to make the website a destination for people. You can do this in several ways. Brenda Novak uses her "fan" section, her "Crimebeat interviews", contests, and news about her annual diabetes auction.

Melissa accomplishes fresh content at misaramirez.com through the newsletter section, Lola Cruz recipes, upcoming appearances, signings, new reviews, classes and the link to The Naked Hero (thenakedhero.com), a site about heroes, heroines, and villains where there is fresh content daily. The Naked Hero is a true destination site on which we, as well as fellow Naked Hero writers, offer writers and readers engaging material for them to keep coming back. Printable items such as writing checklists, inspirational quotes, The Naked Notes, and recipes are all examples of fresh content that will keep people coming back to our site.

If you want your website to be a destination, be creative with your content and think of ways to set yourself apart from the crowd.

Depending upon your personality profile and your strengths, the commitment of creating fresh website content may not work for you. Tonya uses Blogger for her website and blog site (Tonyakappes.blogspot.com). She updates her events and picture pages to keep her readers in the loop about where she'll be and what she's been doing. She keeps the content fresh by posting tri-weekly blogs that encourage other writers. She pays it forward. Her site is geared for her readers and writers, while her grog site The WoMen's Literary Café (www.womensliterarycafe.com) where the content is changed daily to suit the writer's and reader's needs and how everyone can work together as a team in their writing life.

Author Mary Castillo (www.marycastillo.com) does an excellent job of branding herself. She writes stories about Latinas, love, and laughs. Her website has vibrant colors and features the tagline: "Romantic comedies with a Latina twist." When you visit Mary's site, there's no question what she writes.

 **Toolbox Essential**:

Blogging falls under fresh content. Some authors blog. Others do not. Some combine their website's homepage with a simple update blog. Jane Porter (www.janeporter.com) uses her blog on her homepage. Others, like us, are part of a group blog. As long as you have a reason for blogging and have something new to say, or put a new spin on something old, go for it. Blogging on your homepage guarantees fresh content. Just remember: make your blogging relevant!

This works for her. She realizes the reader is vital to her Indie career. She connects with them on all levels of her social media, including her blog site.

Pertinent Information to include on your website:

- Author's bio. Make if fun and show your personality. Professional doesn't mean blah.
- Excerpt of writing. Having an excerpt is an element often missing from author websites. Remember what you're selling! Your publishability. Yes, it can be hard to put yourself out there, but building readership means doing just that. You can also write original work for your website. Think serials, spin-offs, and holiday stories, for example. But remember Editor Toni Plummer's advice and make sure it's polished.
- Contact information. Make sure it's correct!
- Press Kit: 300 dpi photo, long bio short bio (note: bio style should reflect the voice in your book), and agent contact, if applicable.
- FAQ about you as relevant to your writing career: things readers might like to know, the story of your journey, etc. Don't get too personal.
- Current information on your books.
- Links to articles you've written.

Step Three: Keep your audience in mind.

> "If you want readers to remember your name, then give them a reason. good first impression is key. Make certain your website is professional, easy to navigate, and up-to-date. And now that you've sparked an interest with your beautiful website, go beyond with a great blog that is fresh, consistent, and entertaining. Here is where you give readers a reason to come back to you week after week and where you dodge the horrible out of sight, out of mind curse." Author Renee Vincent: www.reneevincent.com

The purpose of a website is to keep your name in your audience's mind.

Judy Taylor, website designer and owner of JT Dataworks (jtdataworks.com), recommends knowing exactly who your audience is.

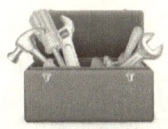 **Toolbox Essential:**

Take the time to visit author websites, noting what you like and don't like about them. Look at colors, fonts, layout, content, categories, photo placement, and anything else that strikes you. Pass this information on to your website designer.

66
99
"An agent who represents writers of dark suspense mysteries is not going too instinctively feel that you are a good candidate to work with her if your site has a perky pink chick lit sort of look. If you are still trying to *find* your preferred, or best, genre then stick to a more generalized, but stylish *writerly* look," says web designer Judy Taylor.

If you are unpublished, your primary audience is agents and editors, while your secondary audience is potential readers.

If you are published, your audience is current and potential readers.

Gear your site toward your intended audience. Fulfill their needs. Whether you include links to buy your book, fun content that will keep them coming back, or something else, give 'em what they want.

Don't let building a website scare you. It can be a fun experience, especially if you keep your goal in mind and work toward it.

Step Four: Knowing the Purpose of Your Website.

- Sell Yourself

Your purpose in having a website, whether unpublished or published, is to feature or "sell" your writing. That is, after all, what you are passionate about and why you are on this publishing path.

A prospective agent, editor, or publisher may find you through your website. What they see there can be the tipping point for them. Based on what they see, will they pursue you as a writer, or cut you lose?

- o One: selling yourself is knowing that a bad website is worse than no website, so make sure you create a professional web presence.
- o Two: make sure your website exemplifies you as a professional writer. Your site is doing more than selling your writing. It's giving a snapshot of your commitment to your craft. You must exhibit proper use of the English language and show your attention to detail. Take yourself seriously as a writer and others will, too.
- o Three: edit your website carefully, always keeping your target audience in mind.
- o Four: choose a website design to match your genre. The visual design of your website should mimic or compliment the style of your writing and the tone of your books. If you write erotica, naked people and a sexy feel are great. For a gritty thriller writer, not so much.
- o Five: dress for the job you want, not the job you have. That saying is applicable to websites, as well. Your job is to sell your personality, or the desired image you are creating, to the public. Build a site that

highlights you AS A WRITER. Sure, being a handsome or pretty person helps, but an interesting life story or a beautiful visage will not sell your book. Dress your website by focusing on your career as a writer, not your pretty face!

Choosing Your Platform

Free Websites verses Custom Website

The type of website you develop depends on your level of comfort with the computer, how 'techy' you are and how much of your own time and/or money you want to put working behind the scenes. Both Free and custom sites have advantages and disadvantages. Read on to figure out what will work for you.

Website Designer Judy Taylor's Big Three Mistakes People Make with Websites:

1. Building your site to suit yourself instead of to attract and hold your audience. To avoid this common problem, always have your target audience in mind when you design and build your site, and ask yourself, "Is this what I want to show them, or is it what they need to see?"

2. Unprofessional, amateur sites. Your site represents YOU and what you are selling. If the site is not professional, then you will not look like a professional.

3. Poor Search Engine Optimization. If your site does not pop up on the top 10 Google results when you type in your name and maybe one other key word like "writer" then you have a serious problem: (unless you have a very common name—if so, you might want to consider a nom de plume.) Be aware however that it can take up to several months for a new site to get on the front page. If your web designer does not specialize in SEO, you also may need to bring a reputable SEO consultant on board. (Caveat—do your homework before hiring, there are WAY more charlatans in this field than good guys.)

"

"Being as techno un-savvy as I am, I hire out the design and upkeep of my main website. It's updated only a few times a year as I get new covers or have something big to announce—updating frequently soon becomes a budget strain. It's a great place to have an extended bio, new releases, backlists, reviews, contact info, and the all-important sign-up for my e-newsletter.

However, I update my blog site almost daily, since it's free for me to do. That's where a reader will find all the need-to-know-now information like upcoming events, and it's also where readers will be able to get to know me on a more personal level. I have links to useful sites, keep a weekday blog, and post what book I'm currently reading among other things. I use Blogger and wouldn't think about changing. It's easy (no HTML code necessary), there are tons of templates, and now that it has the ability to add external pages it has everything I need."
Author Heather Webber/Heather Blake, www.heatherwebber.com

Wordpress

Advantages:

- Gives a person the ability to update and configure their own site. This is particularly beneficial to someone who anticipates adding new content frequently.

- Faster to set up and launch than a custom site.
- Generally less expensive.
- Minimal help needed from a web professional, and usually only at the beginning and/or for customization of the template.
- Site owner is in total control, more or less, of their site after set up is complete.
- Can be styled to look like a custom website, as opposed to a blog.

Disadvantages:

- Wordpress is limited in scope. It's set up to function in a specific way. If those parameters don't work for you, it may be limiting.

- Extreme customization can hike up the price and be problematic.

Blogger

Advantages:
- It's free.
- There are easy step by step instructions.
- You can style it to look like a custom website, or blog site.
- Site owner, and you have complete control and can change site as necessary or as your career changes.

Disadvantages:

- Limited to layout
- Sometimes bloggers have a hard time leaving a comment (rarely happens, but it does).
- It is not easily found by search engines.

Custom Site

Advantages:

- A custom site can be set up so the site owner can manage it his/herself (or not).
- It is infinitely flexible in design and style.

- Usually a better candidate for complete search engine optimization.
- Is not limited by template designs of Wordpress, which means many more specialized features and/or elaborate designs can be integrated into the site.

Disadvantages:

- Generally will cost significantly more to set up and launch.

- Will require the additional cost of updates if author is not able to do this him/herself.

Whether you are in the beginning stages of creating a website, or already have one and have decided to reinvent or redesign it, use this checklist to keep on the right track:

❏ Plan ahead. Figure out your goals for having a website and stick to them as you create design and content.
❏ Know your target audience. Agents? Editors? Readers? Gear content toward that audience.
❏ Create a budget, and then stick to it!
❏ Know your limits and hire a knowledgeable web professional to help you in whatever capacity you've determined.
❏ You should own your domain name, not your web designer! Make sure you do. There are plenty of unscrupulous web masters who have registered domains in their names instead of yours, which makes them the true site owner, not you.
❏ Make sure you have access and control of your domain, hosting control panel, and website server.
❏ Know your access passwords, write them down, and keep them where you can find them. You'll have them if your web master ever keels over, or you have a falling out. Better safe than sorry.
❏ Get verifiable references!!!

“ ” MJ Rose, of AuthorBuzz, says one of the biggest mistakes writers make is spending too much on their website. "It should only be a very small part of your marketing budget. Yes, you need a website but it doesn't need to be complicated. People go to your website after they hear about you or your book. No one wakes up and says I'm going to start searching for websites of authors I never heard of."

Search Engine Optimization (SEA): Imagine a search engine (Google, for example) is a spider, and key words are the flies it's trying to catch. The spider's legs are moving and crawling across the words in the vast database. Those legs glom onto those key words. Your homepage needs to have key words that the search engines recognize. These are the words people use when they search. Use common words. Create categories. Let the spider find your site!

Chapter Five: To Blog or Grog

In This Chapter:
- Know your theme
- Know your audience
- Know your limits and boundaries
- Being free
- Writer's block

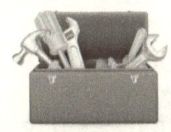 **Toolbox Essential:**

Pay attention to the comments you receive on your blog. Which type of posts attracts the majority of your readers? Which ones get your readers commenting? Is there a pattern? Remember, a memorable blog/grog comes down to great content your audience responds to. Think about them.

"If social media is too 'social' for your personality, if the thought of updating your status on an hourly or daily basis fills you with dread, the next best promotional tool you can use for free is a blog. Consider adding a blog to your site so you can provide rotating content for your readers. You don't have to blog every day. Two or three times a week will be fine. The point is to blog regularly and make sure your readers know you're checking in. Once you set up a pattern, they'll stop by more often to see what you have to say.

The next step is to take advantage of your RSS Feed and put it to good use. A lot of social media sites let you submit your RSS Feed so even without visiting sites like Facebook or Twitter, you can update them each time you blog. Try to submit your RSS feed anywhere you can. It can help bring more name recognition and fresh traffic to your site. Blogging can provide readers with a different platform to get in touch and stay in touch with you. You might not be the only one who doesn't live on a social media site! Some of your readers may prefer to meet up on your blog too. If having your own blog seems too stressful, consider joining a group blog where several authors

participate so the pressure isn't as intense
but you still have an outlet to connect with
readers." ~Leena Hyat,

Blogging is only going to help you if you do it well.
No blog is better than a bad blog. This is not the place to
rant, wax poetic, or otherwise indulge yourself. Use our
guidelines to help you build a better blog.

Know Your Theme

Before you build a blog, you must decide what your
purpose is. Ask yourself these questions:

1. Do I want to be funny and pithy?
2. Do I have enough energy and time to write
   daily, or at least every other day?
   (Remember, a blog without fresh content
   is as stagnant as a mosquito pond)
3. Do I have friends to guest blog?
4. Will I be able to sustain my blog with
   consistent content?
5. Would I prefer to blog alone, or blog with
   buddies?
6. If I blog with others, will I be a leader or a
   follower?
7. If I blog with others, will I be able to set
   boundaries and resolve problems?

Once you've answered these questions, you can
move forward. Remember, you have to decide what your

blog is going to be about—the writing life, genre specific content, book reviews, some element of craft, etc.

When we decided to start a blog together, we structured it so that behind the scenes work was shared equally, we created a private Yahoo group to communicate on, and we decided on a theme we could all embrace and stick with. The Naked Hero has content for readers and writers, thus appealing to a wider audience. It's a destination site for writers seeking information on hero, heroine, and villain archetypes. The Naked Hero tackles the mythic archetypes via pop culture, books, and movies, making it fun and entertaining.

During the big push of electronic publishing and the revolution of the ereader Tonya and Melissa realized there was a need for a website to target everything electronic publishing. People needed to get the low-down on ereaders, self-publishing tips, ways to market and promote as a self published author. They co-founded The Writer's Guide To ePublishing with those elements in mind.

Jungle Red Writers is all mystery, all the time. Six mystery writers stay focused on the theme of their grog. Same with Murder She Writes, a grog with 10 people, all mystery related. Lipstick Chronicles and 14 represent women's fiction/chick lit grogs.

There is no shortage of blogs out there for readers to choose from, so make sure your blog or grog stays focused so readers know exactly what to expect when they stop by.

Know Your Audience

Once you have your theme dialed in, you will know who your audience is. On the flipside, if you know who you want your audience to be, that can help you hone in on an appropriate theme.

Ask the simple question: Who do you want to be reading your blog/grog? Mystery readers? Agents and editors? Romance writers? Men? Women? Mothers? Sci-fi fans? Self-published authors?

Whoever it is, identify them, then gear your site to them. Write about ideas and topics related to your theme that your audience will also be interested in. Blogging/grogging requires commitment. A following is not born overnight. It takes time. Be cognizant of your readers so they know you care about them.

Know Your Limits and Boundaries

We can't reiterate enough the idea that your blog shouldn't be your soapbox. Sure, we have strong opinions on things. Politics, religion, parenting, and the economy all make for interesting discussion. But your blog is to build your writing career. That's it. It serves no other purpose.

Don't be contrary just to be contrary. Don't bait your readers unless that high conflict is part of the daily expectation for your blog.

Do you want to share personal information? Our recommendation would be to keep your personal life...er...personal. Sure, you can mention your family. But do you really want to tell that personal story about the time your neighbor walked up and down the street, stark naked?

We vote, "No!"

Knowing your boundaries will help you stay true to them. What are you going to discuss, and what is off-limits? Knowing this provides you with one more tool to stay focused on your theme and respectful of your audience.

How often are you going to blog? Is everyday too much? Is once a week not enough?

Be Free

We've thrown a bunch of rules at you, and you may be frustrated and wondering what the heck you can write about. Have no fear, as most writers say, ideas are everywhere.

Deciding on your theme, knowing your audience, and being respectful of limits and boundaries makes it all the easier to write freely. Really. Tying topics into your theme, no matter how ridiculous or inapplicable they seem, is actually easier than you might think.

When Melissa gets random emails touting the trials of suffragettes or a spooky Halloween card, she jumps at the chance to use it as a column on The Naked Hero. Suffregettes? Heroines of the past who paved the way for contemporary women. Halloween card? Used as a writing prompt around October 31st.

When Tonya sees a new gadget related to writing or hears of some really cool inspirational success story for writers, she puts that information her back pocket to use for future posts on her blog.

Rules don't mean you can't be creative. They just give you parameters to focus that creativity. If you are having problems coming up related to your theme, Google Alert it! Tonya has several Google Alerts set up for anything and everything electronic publishing.

Go with it!

Writer's Block

Stephen King says writer's block is all hooey. We hear you, Stephen! But we also recognize that sometimes, ideas are slower to come than at other times. Whether you're cooking dinner for the umpteenth time, planting flowers, driving carpool, stuck in commute traffic, or on your way to the Christmas tree farm, ideas abound. Look at life and all your activities through the fresh eyes of a blogger and through the lens of your blog's/grog's theme. Let the creative juices flow.

Enough said.

 **Toolbox Essential:**

Keep a notebook in your car, purse, or briefcase. When you have a random thought, brilliant idea, or otherwise intriguing notion, WRITE IT DOWN! Carpe Bead 'Em...er...Carpe Diem! Don't let fantastic ideas slip away. Grab them before they pop like a bubble, vanishing into thin air.

Chapter Six: Building Your Network: One Nail at a Time

In this chapter:
- What is a network
- Writing organizations
- Critique groups
- Ecentric reader and writer boards (Kindle and Nook Boards)

If you're like most writers, there are two things you do every day after you get up out of bed:

- check your email
- check out your favorite blogs

But wait! Checking emails and reading blogs are great, but you need to do more. We've covered blogging (and how your blog is one many people should be checking in with every morning), but now we're talking about building your network.

Just having a website doesn't cut it these days. Yes, we have our own little world that only we writers understand. But your goal is to build name recognition and find potential readers. That means interacting with other writers and readers in the blogosphere—and beyond.

We're talking about joining actual on-line groups and local writing groups. Trust us, there are plenty out there to fit every personality.

You may be saying to yourself, "Oh no, not me. I'm not a writing group kind of person."

You just hold on to your tool belt. We're going to give you the group networking tools to put in your toolbox—you'll thank us later.

Writing is very lonely. We're sure you've figured out just how lonely it is by the blank stares people give you when you tell them you're a writer. Or how about this one: "Are you published?"

And when you tell them you are on the road to publishing, they tilt their heads and give you the "Huh?" look. Translation: S/he's not really a writer if s/he's not published. Man! Don't you love that look?

The point is, being lonely, especially when you're passionate about something, is no fun. You have to get connected to other writers who understand your passion. Online groups are great for both introvert and extrovert personalities, they help you form connections and broaden your marketing outreach.

Join a group that best suits your writing needs. From there, your level of participation is totally up to you. You can lurk, sitting back and reading what everyone else is doing, or jump right in and comment on all the posts. Or find someplace in the middle.

 **Toolbox Essential:**

Do put yourself out there and comment on some of the posts/topics in the online group. Be a giver, not just a taker. It shows you're a participant, giving you more exposure for your marketing and promotional plan.

What online groups can do for you:

- help you set goals
- make you accountable
- celebrate your successes
- help you overcome your failures
- provide you with information
- help you build the confidence to succeed as a writer
- connect you with like-minded people

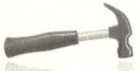

Some of our suggested on-line groups: groups.yahoo.com, groups.google.com, www.gather.com, www.goodreads.com, and www.writing.com.

Navigating Online Groups

No matter what genre you write in, there is a group for you. At Yahoo Groups, for example, just type in your interest. Related groups will come up in the search. Click on them and read what they are about. When you find a group that fits your needs, simply join by clicking on the join button.

One of Tonya's favorite groups is called GIAM , Goal Setting, Inspiration, Amity, Motivation, which she found on the Yahoo group list. At the time she joined, it was a group of twenty women who aspired to be published. They shared everything from information on agents and editors taking pitches, self-;publishing journey, to cheering each other on in contests they entered. This group has expanded and now offers free on-line classes to its members, as well as a website where each member can blog. Membership is still free.

> 66 99 "Fast forward to today and GIAM has four online neighborhoods of published or actively marketing writers, plus another neighborhood (GoPRO) for writers working to finish a manuscript. In addition to our "goals" loops, we offer a class loop, a critique partner matching service, three different writing challenge loops, a chat room, and a new website and Facebook group page. Overall, we're serving nearly 300 members." ~Amy Atwell, founder of GIAM

They are 300 members strong. Just think about that for a second. These are all people who love books and reading, just like you do. Think of all the potential there is to connect with people who will probably be interested in visiting your blog/grog and/or reading your book. Even if you connect with just one person, think of that old Fabergé commercial. It starts with just one person. That person tells someone else. Then they tell one person, and so on....

You might shy away from this type of connection, thinking it's just shameless self-promotion. It's not!

Tonya has become friends with some of the writers in the GIAM group. She's even met a few of them at conferences, traded material to critique, and found people who understand her need to write.

Tonya is also involved with The WoMen's Literary Café (www.womensliterarycafe).

66 99 "We're an online community that bridges the gap between writers and readers with the sole mission of promoting great literature. The WoMen's Literary Café is 'Where readers and authors unite!'

Bridging the gap between the vast community of readers and authors, the WoMen's Lit Cafe offers helpful promotions to authors, reviewers, bloggers, and editors by bridging that bridge to bring readers, authors, and author services together under one umbrella in an easily navigable venue." ~Melissa Foster, founder of WoMen's Literary Café

The authors and bloggers come together and form blog hop when the authors have book launches. The blog hops allows the readers to find new authors, and vice versa.

" "Several years ago I founded The Women's Nest, a social and support site for women. We connect women across the world to share advice, friendship, and a little rejuvenation time. We also offer free resources such as financial, medical, and lifestyle, provided by expert volunteers. The Women's Nest has become such a vital part of many of our members' days that it seemed to make sense to try to provide the same for the writing community.

I've been very lucky with my success, and I've also worked hard to achieve and maintain it. I don't believe success in and of itself is valuable. The value is in what you can give to others because of your success. I have learned a great deal in the past few years about marketing and creating platforms. What I have to give others is the knowledge that I've gained. November 1st, I launched the World Literary Cafe (serving men and women). The World Literary Café is an extension of the The Women's Nest--an online community that bridges the gap between writers and readers with the sole mission of creating a strong community for promoting great literature. The WoMen's Literary Café is quickly becoming the site 'Where readers and authors unite!'"

~Melissa Foster, World Literary Café founder and bestselling author of Megan's Way.

Savvy Author (www.savvyauthors.com) is another phenomenal and inclusive site. It's a community of writers and is bursting with information, blogs, classes, resources, forums, and more. You'll find like-minded people and hone your craft, building your network and making friends along the way.

There are also many genre specific reading groups out there. These groups are about the reader. THE READER! That's who we are spending all our time marketing to. To connect with a reader on a group level is much more personal than signing a book for them at a signings. Believe it or not, readers can be both introverted and extroverted too, but in an online group, you can get into deep discussions about the genre, and books within the genre. Personalities shine in a different way online.

Readers love to connect with authors. Trust us when we say, if they can connect with you on a personal level, they will buy your book.

We pop in at the reader groups we belong to once or twice a week just to keep our names in front of them. We let them know about upcoming contests or news that we've posted on our websites, comment about things going on in their lives, and just stay connected.

If you write in the romance genre, joining Romance Writers of America (RWA) and its online chapters is a great marketing strategy. What better way to meet like-minded people and develop friendships than with a group of writers who write and read exactly what you do.

There is a small fee, but the pay-off outweighs the cost.

Many groups have board elected officials. Tonya has been member liaison with her writers group for years. Why? Because it allows her to meet all the writers and keeps her in-the-know on all things happening in the writing world which she is now part of.

RWA offers great conferences, contests, blog opportunities, forums, a magazine, and classes to help writers develop their writing career. The same is true of other national writing organizations. Check them out!

 **Toolbox Essential:**

Join online writing groups. It doesn't cost you a lot of time and it's a great networking tool. Even the loneliest turtle comes out of his shell every once in awhile.

Another way to connect with writers is through local, unaffiliated writing groups. The Dallas Metroplex area, for example, has Dallas/Ft. Worth Writers, a weekly critiquing group. Smaller cities and towns like Denton, Texas, and Keller, Texas, have their own groups, as well. Cincinnati has Cincinnati Writers Project which is divided into a fiction group and poetry group. Use the internet to search for groups in your area.

These organizations offer many opportunities…and you know what we say about missing those opportunities—DON'T! Speakers, small conferences, and critique groups are just some of what writing groups offer.

Critique Groups. A lot of writers see them as dirty words. Not true!

Being in a critique group will give you the opportunity for honest feedback on your work, will teach you about the craft through the experience of critiquing others, and will give you instant writer friends who will help you promote and market your fabulous new novel.

Tonya's critique groups consists of Heather Webber, Shelley Shephard Grey, Cathy Leggitt, and Hilda Linder-Knepp. Heather, Shelley, and Cathy are all award-winning traditionally published authors, Hilda is aspiring, and Tonya is self-published. They all bring something unique and special to their critique group, even though they are all on different publishing paths.

Conferences are often held by your local writing groups, too. This means exposure to big agents/editors who are looking for that next "big" author.

That just might be you!

When you're published, reader-centric conferences like Fresh Fiction's Readers and Ritas or Lori Foster's Reader Author Get Together, offer you an intimate way to connect with die-hard readers who will proselytize your book to their friends or to anyone who will listen. Whatever your goal, there's a conference for you!

66

99 "What's best is if the writer and I can have a normal, interesting conversation, even about something not related to their work. When they or their agent get in touch with me later, I'll remember the conversation. It's still always going to come down to the actual work. But if I can remember liking the writer and finding him or her interesting, I'm more eager to read their work." Thomas Dunne editor Toni Plummer looks forward to meeting authors while taking pitches at conferences.

Eventually you are going to have to get your novel in front of an agent or editor. What better time to do it than in the safety of that writing group you now belong to?

You can be part of a community which will cheer you on. Your critique group will help you develop your pitch.

Go to that conference and do that pitch. Attend meetings and listen to the featured speakers. Build connections and relationships.

In short, network.

All right, so you may not be ready to pitch. You may not even have your first manuscript finished. But it's never too soon to start the marketing/promotion process.

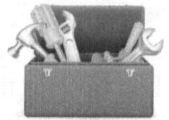 **Toolbox Essential:**

Join Romance Writers of America www.rwanational.org, Mystery Writers of America www.mysterywriters.org, International Thriller Writers, Inc www.thrillerwriters.org, or Sisters in Crime, Inc. www.sistersincrime.org, and then join your local chapters. Each chapter has online groups, as well as the national organization.

66
99
"Volunteering for my local RWA
chapter taught me writing is a business. I
met editors, agents, booksellers and
learned self-promotion is part of the job.
No one will promote your book as well as
you do. It's your baby. Even if you're as
tech-stupid as I am, embrace technology;
it's the tool of your trade." Writer
Margaret Crowley

Volunteer. Conferences are always begging for
people's time. It's good karma to volunteer, and it keeps
you connected. Networking, remember? That's what
we're talking about here.

Do we volunteer? You better believe it!

Keep time at editor pitch appointments? That's us
with the stopwatches. Editors need water? There we are,
Spring Mist bottles in hand.

Don't be afraid to sit outside the room where
agents/editors are taking pitches and be the keeper of the
time. What a great opportunity to meet the agent/editor
without the pressure! It's an opportunity…and we've
already established what we say about
opportunity…DON'T miss out.

Even though Tonya is self-published, she still
belongs to writer's groups and RWA. Your publishing
path doesn't matter, networking, no matter what path you
chose, is very important to your career. Tonya has made
friends with a lot of great editors because she isn't

nervous during the conferences. She keeps the time during pitches and is relaxed. She is building relationships with the authors and agent/editors that are there. You never know when those relationships might come in handy. The publishing world is small.

66
99 "I went to Malice Domestic Convention; I helped assemble goodie bags; went to dinner with 11 great authors and I had a blast interacting with them."
Dru Ann Love~reader

 **Toolbox Essential:**

Volunteering is a great networking tool to keep in your toolbox. It's like a marker. Save it for later use. When you are ready to pitch your novel, you can drop the agent/editor a query and remind them how you met them.

Now that is PRICELESS!

Dru Ann is a reader who stepped out of her comfort zone, went to a conference—alone—and met some of her favorite authors. She even volunteered to stuff swag bags! Now she blogs with them at Cozy Chicks. How cool is she?

Networking, both online and live and in color, is a key piece of your promotion and marketing toolbox. Whether you're a people person or a homebody, there's a group for you. Find it, and then join it.

Kindle and Nook Boards

Every eReader has a forum where readers can connect with readers, authors, and anyone who loves books.

Kindle and Nook are two of the most popular eReaders. They have very active boards.

As a writer, you can go on them and read threads or discussions on successes, failures, tips and tricks. There are some great marketing ideas on those forums. You can also get to know readers, asking them directly what they want.

And yes, you can even pimp your novel.

Remember, you are in charge of your book's marketing and promotions. If you are traditionally published or small press published, you still have to do these activities in order to connect with readers and writers.

Tonya gets on each board once a week. She will put up direct links to her novels so they can be purchased or she will start a thread/forum asking readers what they are reading now.

A simple question gets so many responses. And this has turned into sales for Tonya. The readers will reply back on the thread that they bought Tonya's book or even email her.

Be sure to respond to other threads that you might be interested in. Tonya always posts on threads where readers are asking for new authors or new books to read.

You have to be polite and sincere. Tonya will post the blurb and tell them that she'd love for them to give her novels a chance.

There are rules that have to be followed or the forum moderator will call you out on it, so be sure to read all the rules that are listed.

Chapter Seven: What Marketing and Promotional Tools Do You Want to Hang on Your Rafters?

In this chapter:
- Fangirl (or boy) versus stalker
- Educating your taste
- Save the swag

Fangirl (or boy) Versus Stalker

We believe in visiting your favorite blogs, and visiting often. Not only do you need to read what bloggers are posting, you need to comment. But know there is a difference between being a fangirl (or boy) and stalker (this comes from personal experience!). We don't want you calling us in the middle of the night from your local jail because you've gone to the dark side!

Commenting on blogs is a great networking tool. If you are consistent, the author of the blog will begin to recognize your name and see that you are there for them.

As members of a great grogs (thenakedhero.com and theworldliterarycafe.com), we love to see the same visitors over and over again. We view it as building a community. We also believe in paying it forward. We've had some of our loyal readers write guest blogs for us, allowing them to showcase their own blogs, books, and personalities.

This brings over their readers which could turn into potential readers for you.

Good karma, remember?

 **Toolbox Essential:**

When you comment on a blog, be sure to leave your website URL. The other bloggers will be able to click on your name and it will take them straight to your website.

Just to reiterate, don't do anything illegal or crazy, just get your name out there, be seen, heard, and begin to develop relationships with other bloggers.

The purpose? You're building your networking community from the ground up. When you're ready to promote that big novel, your peeps will be in place.

Educating Your Taste

Being a fangirl (or boy) and consistently visiting your favorite author blogs will help you learn the different ways authors have of building buzz for their work, consequently educating your taste about what you think will work for you. Many host contests through their posts or direct you to their main website. They will even send you to another blog where they are guest blogging. This is the author's way of saying, "I'll scratch your back if you scratch mine," a theory we'll talk about later in the *Tricked Out Toolbox*.

In true fan fashion, make sure you enter every contest your favorite authors host. You will begin to get all sorts of items we like to call swag.

Be diverse by following all kinds of authors. You don't only have to follow authors you know and like. Be an equal-opportunity fan. When you visit authors in your genre, you will find all sorts of new ideas for when you begin to market yourself, but you may find great ideas outside your genre, too.

Save the Swag!

> "The items that work for me are my hot pink pens. I started passing them out at my first signing and had so many responses from readers that I kept ordering them. The majority of my readers that e-mail me with compliments on my books usually comment on how much they love the pens." Jules Bennett, www.julesbennett.com

> "The best marketing tool I've ever found is...to be yourself. Open up to readers. Engage them without it being all about YOU. It can be a huge turn-off if all

readers hear from you is about you, you, you—your books, your schedule, your promo. I get a lot out of just visiting with readers, talking about books we've read and enjoyed, but also talking about life, kids, husbands, vacations, etc... I'm a real person, and those oh-so-fabulous readers are real people.

Social networks are fabulous for this, as long as you're not constantly pushing for a book sale. I've also found that bookmarks or magnets are a big hit with readers who request them."
Author Lori Foster, www.LoriFoster.com

 **Toolbox Essential:**

We love this idea from YA Author Melissa Walker, melissacwalker.com: "One big thing I did was to send copies of my books to high school newspapers for review. Publishers never think to do this but it's instant audience access, and almost ALL of the newspapers printed reviews. COOL!"

How brilliant is this?

Bookmarks, post cards, pens, book plates, magnets, signed books... You name it and we'll lay odds that it's being given away on a daily basis by an author somewhere. As you gather these materials, you will start to get a sense of what you think will work for you and your book promotion needs.

They can get pricy, so know your purpose in creating them and how you'll use them before you hit the PayPal button and deplete your bank account. Try to create products that will grow with you as your career moves from unpublished to published.

Think about your PR personality, whether you're an introvert or an extrovert, and choose materials that fit your plan. For example, if you plan to go to book fairs, book signings, and conferences, bookmarks and postcards are tangible products to hand out with or without your book. They can be mailed to friends, family, and your growing mailing list. Be creative by making your postcards something people want to keep. We've talked about including recipes, but you could go a different direction. Include inspirational quotes, a craft idea, cool information related to a theme or topic in your book (WWII aircraft facts, for example), or whatever else sparks your imagination.

Business cards are another item to keep constant in your toolbox as your career grows and changes. They can be passed out at conferences, speaking engagements and events, and to people you meet on airplanes, trains, and in the supermarket. (Incorporate QR codes onto these products; more about that later!) However, if you feel you'll only occasionally need business cards, bookmarks with your contact information may be the better option.

Melissa has had wonderful luck putting recipes on postcards. "Recipes tie into the Lola Cruz Mystery Series since the family owns a Mexican restaurant. I like the idea of giving away something that people have a reason to keep. A delicious recipe is the perfect example of something people turn to, over and over." ~ Melissa

A staple for everyone!
Spanish Rice

Also called Sopa de Arroz, this dish can be made with fresh onions, garlic, and tomatoes, or you can do it the simplified "Lola" way.

2-4 Tablespoons oil
1 cup Long Grain white rice
1 6 oz. can tomato sauce
1/2 tsp. garlic powder
1/2 tsp. onion powder
[the seasoning Adobo can be substituted for the garlic and onion]
1 tsp. salt, to taste
2 cups water or chicken broth

Directions:
Heat oil in heavy saucepan. Add rice and brown. Stir in 3/4 of the can of tomato sauce [add more if you prefer moister rice, less if you prefer it less tomatoey and drier]. Add water or broth, garlic and onion powder, and salt. Bring to a boil. Reduce heat, cover, and simmer approximately 20 minutes or until liquid is absorbed.

A Little Flavor of Lola: "When I was fourteen years old, I snapped pictures of Jack Callaghan doing the horizontal salsa in the back seat of a car with Greta Pritchard. That's when I knew for sure I'd grow up to be a private eye."

--From Living the Vida Lola, St. Martin's Press January 20, 2009

Buen Provecho!   http://www.misramirez.com

Toolbox Essential:

Start a swag collection. You heard right. Collect and save swag from other authors. When you are budgeting and planning your own swag development and giveaways, look through the things you've collected to garner ideas that will work for you.

Tonya has had success with promotional and marketing items that go along with the theme of her book.

Something Spooky This Way Comes
Available October 24, 2010

Carpe Bead 'Em
Available May 23, 2011

The Ladybug Jinx
Available July 4, 2011

Tonya Kappes, the queen, princess, and jester in her family of 4 boys, 2 dogs, and best friend husband, is the author of two novels, Carpe Bead 'Em and The Ladybug Jinx. She writes contemporary women's fiction and humorous cozy mysteries with quirky characters and quirkier situations. Find out what's going on with Tonya at www.tonyakappes.com.

She attached small bags of candy corn to go along with the Halloween theme of *Something Spooky This Way Comes*, the anthology in which her story, "Masked Souls" (Turquoise Morning Press, Oct. 2010), appears.

Tonya also attached a small bag of sand on her novel postcards for Carpe Bead 'em where she won the number one postcard by an author at The Lori Foster's Reader and Writer Get Together 2011.

Visiting other authors' websites and being attentive to their giveaways and swag educates your taste. See Chapter Nine for more about promotional items.

 **Toolbox Essential:**

Websites that give-away free books:

- Booksonthehouse.com

- Bookdivas.com

- Goodreads.com

- Freshfiction.com

- Christianbook.com

- Harperteen.com

- Freebookfriday.com

- The-cheap.net (for Nookbook)

- Kindlenationdaily.com (for Kindle)

- Kindleonthecheap.com (for Kindle)

- Ereadernewstoday.com

Be sure to check your favorite author sites because they are always giving away free advanced reading copies (ARCS), or swag.

"This may sound like a very strange story, but it's because of Jane Porter's books—and the shove of my husband that I began my writing career. I could really relate to Jane's books and I had that need to connect to this author.

Every day, I made sure I commented on Jane's blog. I entered every contest she had and followed her wherever she guest blogged. I know—stalker! She would send out a call for anyone who wanted some Jane swag to email her (she didn't call it swag, but that's what it was). You know I was on it! I even stalked the mailman during this time. She sent the neatest stuff: fingernail files, water bottles, pens, mirrors, letter openers, and much more. She even mailed me a Christmas card that year. I taped it up on the mantel like she was family. This also happened to be the time I finished my very first novel and started to send out queries.

Jane knew my name, but not me or my writing. I joined a grog and she stopped by to comment a few times. It was like a celebrity had contacted me. I even printed it out on the computer. Can you say stalker?

Fast forward a few years. I see Jane is coming to town for a book fair. I send her an email telling her I'd like to take her to dinner and ask her what her plans are. She says she doesn't have any plans or a place to stay. Oh yeah! You know what I'm thinking. And, yes, I did it. Jane stayed at my house for two nights. It was the most amazing experience I've ever had as a reader and an author. And it's all because I started to follow her blog.

Most importantly, I made a wonderful friend. It's a fine line between stalked and fangirl. I like to think I'm a fangirl extraordinaire." ~Tonya

Tonya's story might not be how you'd handle meeting your favorite author, but she has an extroverted personality. She learned how to communicate with readers by Jane's example and now she puts it into action.

She got great marketing ideas by visiting Jane's blog and receiving some great promotional items. Granted some of the items are a little out of Tonya's budget, but she's filed the information away in her toolbox for the day she can afford that kind of swag.

So remember, keep all the promotional materials you collect from other authors. You'll be educating your taste as you develop your own plan.

 **Toolbox Essential:**

When you are visiting blogs, click on other commenters' names so you can see what their website or blog is. You might find a new person to follow. AND remember it's networking, no matter what your PR personality is.

Bottom line? Networking, a crucial part of marketing, starts long before you finish that first novel.

Chapter Eight: Become a Social Contractor

In this chapter:
- A Tech-Heavy World
- Facebooking it
- The lowdown on Twitter
- Connecting with others

A Tech-Heavy World

In today's publishing industry, more and more marketing department budgets are being chopped and skewered—and they were never well-stocked in the first place. What this means to you, the writer, is that the burden of marketing and promotion falls largely on your shoulders.

You may be thinking that your publisher's marketing department will set up book signings, send out promotional items to booksellers and reviewers, send a photographer to take your author photo, and send you on an all-expense-paid-book signing trip.

We hate to burst your bubble, but you have some major stars in your eyes!

We thought the same things, but boy, were we wrong. Yes, the publisher will send ARCs out for review or a self-published author will send out their own ARCs, though there are no guarantees a book will actually get reviewed. Realistically, that's about all you can expect. Any more than that is icing on the cake...or it means you're Janet Evanovich, Harlan Coben, or Elizabeth

George, so what the heck are you doing reading this book anyway?

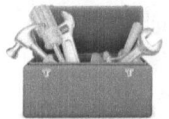 **Toolbox Essential:**

The Internet is the introvert's best friend. You can network to your heart's content, all from the comfort of your computer keyboard.

It's great for extroverts, too! Remember to identify your strengths and play to them.

Enter the Internet. A few short years ago, getting your name in front of a lot of people was challenging. Not so in today's tech-heavy world. Twitter and Facebook make it easy to establish almost instant "friends," which, for an author, translates to a captive audience for promotion.

While there are many social networks (listed at the end of this chapter), we're delving into the top two—and the most time-efficient social networking venues for writers.

" "One of the best things an author can do before, during and after a new book release is to take advantage of the several social media options available today. Social media is generally free and helps put your name, your website and title of your book in front of literally thousands of readers. Sites such as Facebook, Twitter, LinkedIn, YouTube and others can also help drive a considerable amount of new visitors to your site, some of whom may return again. However, it's not just a matter of signing up on a social media website. The only way it can benefit you is if you engage the readers in some way.

If you're a newbie and not ready to jump in at the deep end, start by just checking in to see what your friends are up to. Leave a brief comment like 'Congrats' or 'Happy Birthday' where appropriate, comment on someone else's comment or simply hit the 'Like' button on someone else's status. It puts your name on their radar and gives them a small taste of what interests you. Once you get the hang of it, you can progress to updating your own status and letting friends know what you're up to. Each time you engage

people, you're reminding them of who you are, what you write and where they can find out more about you and your books. Whether your aim is to promote your website or get the buzz going about your new book, social media is one of the best, free methods of promotion today."
Leena Hyat,
www.authorsoundrelations.com

Facebooking It

Facebook is a very valuable tool for writers. Be forewarned, however. There is a right way and a wrong way to promote and market yourself on this networking platform. Do
it right and you're on your way to building a solid fan-base. Do it wrong and you risk alienating people.

Pros of Facebook:

- It's FREE!!
- Your profile page is a bull's eye into your brand.

- You can 'LIKE' reading/writing groups, your desired audience.
- You can connect with other writers.
- It is an instant forum for research: pose a question on your wall about your work-in-progress and get immediate answers.
- Allows you to grow your fan base.
- Lets you reach a large group of readers at one time (posting book trailers, reviews, blurbs, and more).
- It's set up to post mini-feeds to your blog posts.
- Allows you to 'TAG' other people, so what you write can appear on their walls.
- Lets you send event information to a specific group of people (guest blogs, book signings, parties, etc).

Cons of Facebook:

- Can be a time-sucker if you don't use it effectively.
- You can inadvertently expose too much personal information on your page.
- May expose your computer to viruses.
- May reintroduce you to long-lost pals. We aren't saying don't, just don't forget this is a FREE marketing tool for you. Use the phone to connect with lost friends, or create a Facebook page separate from your author persona.

- Can lure you into the mind-numbing, albeit fun, games.
- It's a fine line between professional and unprofessional. It's easy to cross, so be careful!

We use Facebook to connect with readers and writers. Whenever we have a question or need a favor, we can always count on our cyber-friends to step up to the plate and help. For example, while we were writing this book, we posted an all-call to authors on our status: "What promo/marketing tools work for you, and what don't?" The responses were incredible—and are still trickling in. Once on Facebook, always on Facebook.

When Melissa needed ideas for titles for the third Magical Dressmaking Mystery, she turned to her Facbook friends. The response list was long, and almost all the suggestions were fantastic. One friend suggested Deadly Patterns—the winning title. As a result, she has a character named after her in the book.

Remember, if you want to use Facebook for personal use (as opposed to marketing, we recommend setting up a personal page that is separate from your author/fan page. Having a dedicated page just for devoted readers is the best way to stay connected with them.

~ Melissa and Tonya

How to Use Facebook as a Marketing and Promotional Tool

Tonya changes her status twice a day, posting about something writing-related. "Before I self-published my first novel, I posted questions about research, put up pictures I took with other writers or at writing events, posted links to guest blog posts, and put up inspirational quotes.

I always send a personal note to people who respond to me. It's human nature to want to be acknowledged. Remember how you used to feel when you received a handwritten letter or thank you note in your mailbox? The handwritten letter is a dying art, but personal connection—and our need for it—lives on. Communicate with other people directly. Respond to their comments. Build relationships. This is how you connect with readers and writers on Facebook.

A month before my debut novel, *Carpe Bead 'Em*, I began to add new items to my Facebook page. Up went status reports of my edits, novel cover, blogs, and photos of places I envisioned in my novel. I started contests linked to my website in order to generate more traffic there." ~Tonya

The potential of Facebook is phenomenal. Don't discount it.

 **Toolbox Essential:**

Do not put in your status that you are gone on vacation or out to dinner. It's a proven fact: burglars are cruising Facebook for those status updates.

One big no-no on Facebook for any public figure is posting too many personal pictures. Yes! Readers are curious about you. They may even see you as a celebrity of sorts.

But keep your personal life as separate from your professional writing life as possible.

Sure, you can post a few pictures to satisfy readers' desire to know more about you on a personal level, but don't give away the kitchen sink. There are crazies out there. Fangirl verses stalker. It's a fine line, remember?

The Lowdown on Twitter

" Cozy mystery writer, Lorraine Bartlett, believes social networking sites like Facebook and Twitter are the best use of time and money. It costs "nothing but your time. You'll save thousands of dollars (compared to attending conferences where often all you get is a big credit card bill) and connect with far more people."

Twitter is a fast-paced free social network that requires little time. Harness the power and you're in for a wild ride.

Twitter is a great way to talk about your ideas, but consistency is key. Be personable, don't just self-promote. Pithy is good. Humor is great. Twitter is a powerful social networking tool. Just use it wisely.

Pros of tweeting:

- It's fast and furious.
- You write snippets of 140 characters or less.
- It's easy to link to writer sites or reader sites.
- It can be a great platform to promote your novels.
- It provides instant gratification.
- People give quick responses to research questions.
- It can connect you with high profile people.

Cons of tweeting:

- Like Facebook, Twitter can be a time-sucker if you're not careful.
- It's a way to connect with people, but finding those people takes time.
- It's difficult to isolate and connect with people who have specific reading interests.
- Keeping your posts to 140 characters or less can be tough.
- Everybody's gaming it, so standing out in a crowded room is challenging.

How to Use Twitter:

- Set up a free account by logging in. Choose a username and password.
- Upload an image for your profile and fill out other profile information.
- Include KEY WORDS in your bio. Examples: Name of book series, interests, the fact that you're a writer...anything that someone else might search.
- Begin tweeting.
- Shorten any links you post in your Tweets. Go to a URL shortening site, enter the full URL of your link, and Voila!, it'll be shortened to something manageable in Twitter. Shorten your URL at: TinyURL.com, xr.com, Tiny9.com, bitly.com.
- Use the search bar to find people with similar interests, people who read an author you liken yourself to, etc, and FOLLOW them.
- When people follow you, you'll be notified. Thank them for following!
- Use hashtags in your tweets. Tonya will tweet about her novel set in Grandberry falls: #smalltown @tonyakappes11 Is it #love or just the spirit of #Christmas? http://amzn.to/vKUdzN #kindle. She uses Bitly.com to shorten the Amazon link,

then does another tweet for Nook readers. Hashtags put you into the twitter feeds of popular subjects. She does this for all her tweets. Other common hashtags: #paranormalromance #paranormal #cozymystery #amwriting #giveaway.

Tweet, and be happy.

Toolbox Essential:

Remember to give back! Comment on other people's Facebook statuses, re-tweet other people's tweets, thank people for the follows, and comment back on Twitter. It's all about karma! The more you give to the writing and reading community, the more you will get out of it.

"Think back to your marketing plan. You should have compiled a list of dream readers (your target audience. Now is when you get creative with that list. Use social media to your advantage.

I wanted readers of Stephanie Plum to venture out and give my Lola Cruz Mysteries a try. I searched

Stephanie Plum on Twitter, found people who love Janet Evanovich's series, and started Tweeting with them. I'm getting exposure for my series and connecting with like-minded people at the same time." ~Melissa

For A Magical Dressmaking Mystery series, she created a twitter account for Melissa Bourbon (her pen name: twitter.com/melissabourbon) and has just begun searching seamstresses, sewers, dressmaking, fashion Project Runway, Kate Collins, Maggie Sefton (and other books/authors similar to hers), etc. She's following them, tweeting about sewing and such, and is steadily garnering a Twitter following.

Connecting with Others

You can find agents and editors on social media outlets. Sometimes agents and editors will throw a curve ball at their followers/friends. We have several friends who have responded to an agent's status. One agent, for example, posted: "Send me a query letter. I'll take the first five I get."

What a great opportunity, and one you'll miss, if you're not a social networker.

One summer, Melissa's kids started a blog called A Kid's Cooking Challenge, challenging themselves to cook using Jamie Oliver recipes for as long as possible. "I helped them start a Twitter account. We tweeted and Jamie Oliver got wind of their blog, commented on it, tweeted with them, and then featured them in his monthly newsletter. Social networking works!

Final Thoughts

You can eliminate a lot of the time-suck by being efficient about your social networking. Most social media outlets can be updated through your smart phone, hand-held device, or tablet. We've found this to be a great tool for our toolbox! Between them, Melissa and Tonya have nine children. "We are each always tending to their needs so we have to use our time wisely and update our status when we are in car-line, waiting on our kids to come out of extra-curricular activities, sitting at basketball games, watching marching band..." Tonya has even been known to take her phone in the bathroom to update because it saves time. TMI?!

Another tip: Use alternative Twitter interfaces to schedule your updates. Set up automatic tweet updates and/or manage multiple Twitter accounts using these Twitter Interfaces:

- Tweetdeck
- Seesmic
- Twhirl
- Twaiter
- HootSuite

"Every Sunday night, I schedule my tweets through Socialooomph (because it's free). It does take about half an hour to do, but it's definitely worth it. I schedule tweets for every fifteen minutes each day. And it's not all about me or writing. I will put on quotes, tweet upcoming events, other author friend's writing news, etc...At the end of each day, and I go back on twitter and look at the mentions of my name. I will then retweet a sincere thank you to whoever retweeted my tweets. Good networking!" ~Tonya

Now it's time to hammer down your social media and what is best for your PR personality.

Other social networks that might work for you and your personality:

- LinkedIn www.linkedin.com
- Goodreads www.goodreads.com
- Shelfari.com
- Library Thing www.librarything.com
- Book Crossing www.bookcrossing.com
- Revish www.revish.com
- Reader 2 www.reader2.com
- Tumblr www.tumblr.com
- Stumbled Upon.com
- Yahoo Groups groups.yahoo.com
- Google Groups groups.google.com
- Blogtalkradio.com

 **Toolbox Essential:**

If you haven't Googled yourself, do! Sign up for Google Alerts. Anytime someone posts your name or book title on the internet, Google will send you an email and URL where to find it. This is important for two reasons.

One: If you know who's reading and writing about your book, you can stop by, surprise the blogger and his/her readers, and comment.

Two: There are many piracy sites out there giving books away for free. Demonics and 4share are two examples. Google Alerts keeps you abreast of everything related to you and your book in cyberspace.

As Sir Francis Bacon famously said, "Knowledge is power."

Chapter Nine: Promotional Items for your Toolbox

In this Chapter:
- Promotion and Marketing on a Dime
- Blog/Grog Gear
- Giving your promo materials to Editors/Agents

We've covered how to effectively market yourself online:
- Have a basic website
- Join writing groups
- Visit favorite blogs daily and comment
- Join (or create) a blog/grog
- Join the social media craze

It doesn't matter if you are starting to write now, looking for an agent, looking to publish through a publisher, or self publishing. it's never too early to start marketing and promoting.

Build your fan base now, and when that book deal materializes, you'll have your audience ready and waiting. If you already have a book deal, a book, or many books, it's never too late to start thinking like a PR pro.

Now let's get to the FUN STUFF!

It's time to take some of the tools you now have in your toolbox and use them to create promotional materials. They can be a blast to create. Think outside the box and use your brand and tagline to help get you noticed in the writing and reading community.

Promotion and Marketing on a Dime

Stainless steel appliances in a kitchen, or knock-offs—just as pretty, but half the cost. Which would you choose? We vote for the knock-offs. We're all about budget and we believe in promotion and marketing on a dime (see Appendix F: Marketing Budget Worksheet).

If you are Microsoft Office, Pages, or Photoshop savvy, there are templates and products to make your own promo materials. If you're not techy, the cost-savings may not be worth the time investment. But if you are able to design your own products, go for it!

This is the business card Tonya created before she was even finished with her first novel. By using the tools in her toolbox, she was able to include her tagline, website URL, and grog URL. She even utilized the back of the card by using her tagline concept and coming up with a quirky drink recipe called Hillbilly Punch.

Hillbilly Punch

4 cups ice cubes
1 fluid ounce white rum
1 fluid ounce peach schnapps
1 fluid ounce amaretto liqueur
1 1/2 cups cranberry juice cocktail, chilled
1 cup lemon-lime flavored carbonated beverage, chilled

*Fill a (1 quart) canning jar with ice.
*Measure in rum, peach schnapps and amaretto liqueur.
*Pour in cranberry juice until glass is 3/4 full.
*Fill with lemon-lime soda.

If you decide to have promotional materials printed for you, take a little time to do your homework. There are many printing companies. Most have specials. Find out who's offering what and make your most cost-effective decision. Most of these websites offer free shipping or will send you weekly HEAVILY discounted items. Vistaprint, for example, offers free products every week.

Another promotional item we have used is website postcard, clearly stating The Naked Hero platform: Hero/Heroine/Villain Archetypes, giving a snapshot of what the site offers.

We featured our grog members' personal websites (at the time) and, again, we utilized recipes, placing them on the back (clearly, we're all about the food and drink!).

Every Goddess loves a *Naked Lady Cocktail*:

1 2/5 parts BACARDI Superior Rum
1 2/5 parts Noilly Prat Rouge (sweet vermouth)
1/5 part Apricot brandy
1/5 part Pomegranate Grenadine
1/5 part Freshly squeezed lemon juice
Cubed ice

Directions:

Lemon zest to garnish
Put all ingredients into a shaker
Throw in the ice
Shake that baby until the outside of the shaker gets very cold
Double strain into a chilled or frozen glass
Garnish with the lemon zest

Blog/Grog Gear

Remember, your goal with promotional items is to keep your name (or your blog/grog's name) in your readers' and writer friends' consciousness.

We promote The Naked Hero just as much as we
promote our books. Why? Because name recognition
happens organically when people visit your website over
and over and over. The Naked Hero is a destination site
for anyone who loves books, reading, writing, and/or
wants to learn more about hero, heroine, and/or villain
archetypes. When they visit our site, they see our books,
front and center. Well, actually, they're scrolling along in
the right sidebar, but you get the drift.

We sell t-shirts, mousepads, mugs, and other
products. We also wear our t-shirts when we go to
conferences or give workshops. Use Photoshop to create
your designs (or whatever design application you are
comfortable with), then upload to one of the online store
sites. It took about one hour and, Voila!, Our online store
was born.

 **Toolbox
Essential:**

Nuts or Screws? Use the Killer Marketing Plan sheet

(See Appendix A) in the back of the book. It's a great

tool to use when you are trying to decide what

promotional items are going to work for you and your

personality.

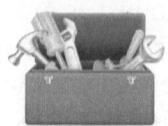 **Toolbox Essential:**

Be creative with your promotional items. Everyone does bookmarks. Are you a beader? Maybe you should do book thongs.

Think outside the box! Tonya had return address labels made up with her tagline and website address. She bought single-serve coffee packets in bulk at her local warehouse market. She put a label on the back of each of those coffee pouches and handed them out at a book signing. Now that's creative!!

Carpe Bead 'Em
Available May 23, 2011
Tonyakappes.com

Once you have swag boasting your name and information so stalkers…er…fangirls/boys can find you on the web, what do you do with it?

Remember those conferences, groups, book signings we recommend you attend. These provide great opportunities for you to leave your products sitting out on the promotional tables they have for writers and readers. Some conferences offer swag bags. They actively seek promotional items to put in those bags. Send your stuff! Better yet, volunteer to stuff bags.

In Leena's Goodie Room (www.authorsoundrelations.com), Lee puts together promotional and marketing material for readers that send requests and it's free. All you have to do is send her what you want in the bags. Your material is put in with a lot of other authors' materials, but your name is getting out there reaching potential readers.

Bottom line…get your promo materials in front of other readers and writers to start building name recognition.

Giving Your Promo Materials to Editors/Agents:

If you've signed up for an agent/editor pitch appointment where you will pitch your book at a conference, don't be afraid to pass along your promo materials. Your goal: to get a request for a submission. Having a business card, bookmark, recipe card, or coffee pouch to give them can help keep you in their memory.

The back of a business card is a great place for the agent/editor to jot down a quick note about you after you leave, particularly important if they are interested in your book or responded to your pitch. It can be a reminder to them of your awesomeness!

As your career grows and changes, so will your swag. You'll create items which include your book titles, upcoming release dates, and more. More on that later in Chapters Ten and Sixteen.

Some printing companies to look at for business cards, bookmarks, postcards, etc:

- Vistaprint.com
- NextDayFlyers.com
- GotPrint.net
- psprint.com
- Printplace.com
- printrunner.com
- printingforless.com
- idsketch.com
- mmprint.com
- printingblue.com
- cafepress.com

- printfection.com
- spreadshirt.com
- PrintMojo.com
- e-shirt.com
- zazzle.com
- pistolclothing.com
- sonicshack.com
- fibers.com
- businesscardland.com
- 123print.com
- iprint.com

 Keep in mind that this won't work for all editors and agents. Some prefer correspondence via email and just can't keep all the promo items they receive. Agent Holly Root says, "I like bookmarks...for published authors anyway. For unpublished authors looking for representation, I'd much rather see a great query/pages than killer swag."

Ultimately, it all comes down to the book you've written, so use the Killer Marketing Plan worksheet and your Marketing Budget worksheet (see Appendix A and

Appendix F) to make the most informed choices as you spend your promotion dollars.

 **Toolbox Essentials:**

Remember, your marketing plan is fluid. You should revise your Action Plan Worksheet as your career changes. Creating promotional products that can grow with your career is a wise decision.

 **Toolbox Essential:**

There are scads of promotional materials out there. Use this list to get you started with the basics:

- Business cards
- Stationary
- Return Address labels
- Post cards
- Pens

- Post-it notes
- Mugs
- Bookmarks

- Recipe cards

Section Two: Using Your Toolbox to Frame and Finish Your House

Up until now, we've discussed elements of marketing and promotion relevant to both unpublished and published authors. But what do you do once you get "the call"? How do your marketing and promotion efforts change and become more focused?

Hopefully, you've laid out solid blueprints and have a sturdy foundation on which to build. Now it's time to narrow your focus as you gear up for the next step in your writing career.

Chapter Ten: Promotional Material after the Call

In this chapter:
- Updating Promotional Materials
- Book trailers
- A Quickie Book Trailer Tutorial

Updating Promotional Materials

It's really important to update all of your promotional materials once you sell, have a book cover, blurbs, and reviews. If you're chomping at the bit, but don't have a cover yet, be creative. When her short story, "Masked Souls," sold, Tonya made promo materials before she had a cover. She got creative and focused on the theme of Halloween.

She added a recipe on the card (you know how we dig those recipes!), which makes it more likely readers will keep the card around longer. At a local event Tonya attended, she handed out goodie bags with the recipe card and one ingredient from the recipe; her target readers loved it. Each walked away with a new recipe and an ingredient they didn't have to buy, plus all of the book information for the upcoming release.

For "Another Quirky Christmas," she included the cover on the promotional card she created, along with the book release information and her contact information on the back.

You may need to rework your business cards once you're agented and/or have sold. Make sure they are professional, but reader friendly. Remember, know your audience. You are now trying to reach and connect with your target readers instead of agents and editors. Include your name, website(s)/blog (s), book title and/or series title, and a tagline.

Include your book blurb on the back of your business card and/or postcards. Use what you have and get creative. Your goal is to keep your name and book in front of your reader.

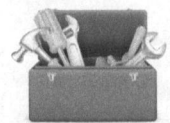 **Toolbox Essential:**

Recipes are a great marketing idea for your toolbox, even if you DON'T cook. Readers collect and keep recipe cards! This means they are keeping your name in front of them.

Tonya Kappes

Tonyakappes.com

Quirky Christmas Cookie Recipe
(red velvet cookies)

*One pouch sugar cookie mix
*1/3 cup unsweetened cocoa
*1/4 cup butter softened
*1/4 cup sour cream
*1 tablespoon red food color
*3/4 cup cream cheese frosting from can
*1 egg

Directions:

Heat oven to 375°F. In large bowl, stir cookie mix, cocoa, butter, sour cream, food color and egg until soft dough forms. Roll dough into 1-inch balls; place 2 inches apart on ungreased cookie sheet. Bake 8 to 9 minutes or until set. Cool 2 minutes; remove from cookie sheet to wire rack. Cool completely, about 15 minutes. Frost cooled cookies with frosting. Sprinkle with mix. Store tightly covered at room temperature.

Another Quirky Christmas

Believe Anthology
ISBN# 978-1935817277

Be sure to check out Tonya's website for news, upcoming events, and contests!!

Tonya Kappes

Tonya Kappes, the queen, princess, and jester in her family of 4 boys, 2 dogs, and best friend husband, is the author of two novels, Carpe Bead 'Em and The Ladybug Jinx, as well as Masked Souls short story in Something Spooky This Way Comes Anthology. She writes contemporary women's fiction and humorous cozy mysteries with quirky characters and quirkier situations.

**Masked Souls,
Something Spooky This Way Comes
ISBN-13: 9781935817253**

**Another Quirky Christmas
Believe Anthology
ISBN-978-1935817277**

**Tricked Out Toolbox
available April 4, 2011**

**Carpe Bead 'Em
available May 23, 2011**

**The Ladybug Jinx
available July 4, 2011**

Tonyakappes.com

The Tricked-Out Toolbox

Be effective with space. Tonya killed two birds with one stone. For *Believe*, an anthology with her story, "Another Quirky Christmas," she included a new recipe on the front along with a picture of the book cover. On the back she included her bio and listed all her books with ISBN numbers and release dates. She even attached a nutcracker ornament she got fairly cheap from Oriental Trading since there was a nutcracker in her story. Tonya thinks outside the box.

Once Melissa's second book was near the release date, she created a second recipe card. This time, she included both of the book covers in the series, as well as the ISBN numbers, a brief excerpt, and contact information.

She also continues to include recipes mentioned in the Lola books in a recipe section of her website. Remember, fresh content! You want your promo materials to work for you by getting people to come to your website. Once there, your excerpts and writing will sell your books.

Available February 2, 2010
ISBN-10: 0312384033
ISBN-13: 978-0312384036
Minotaur Books

A Lola Cruz Recipe: # 2

Lola's recipe for irresistable Margaritas is on the back!
(Bonus recipe: Salsa Borracha, perfect with margaritas)

A taste of Lola:

"I can't even begin to count the number of times my grandmother told me that she would die a happy woman if only I'd join the Order of the Benedictine Sisters of Guadalupe and live a chaste and holy life. To which I always nodded, smiled, and said, "I want you to die happy, Abuela, pero I'm not going to become a nun." There were several problems with me and a pious life. If you asked my mother, she'd say I'd sinned over and over and over again, beginning with premarital intercourse (which she suspected but had no actual proof of), and ending with my job. In my mother's eyes, being a detective necessitates questionable actions and an 'ends justifies the means' philosophy."

136

Include leftover promo materials from your pre-call days in swag giveaways/goodie bags during your blog or book tours, and/or give them away with contest.

> " "I often hear authors say, 'Bookmarks and logoed trinkets don't sell books.' But that's not their job. Bookmarks, postcards, pens, key chains, etc. should help reinforce your pen name and encourage readers to check out your website. Your website is your primary marketing tool, with its book covers, blurbs, excerpts, and purchase links. The only promotional handout I've found that has a good chance of directly selling a book is an excerpt or first chapter booklet." Marcia James, www.marciajames.net

Marcia James is right. Promo materials aren't going to make the reader buy your book, but they will put, and ideally keep, your name in front of them. If one out of ten readers makes it to your website as a result of your promo materials, or stops when they see your book at the bookstore or at a web store, your promo materials have done their job.

Walt Disney said, "Somehow I can't believe that there are any heights that can't be scaled by a man who knows the secrets of making dreams come true. This special secret, it seems to me, can be summarized in four

C's. They are curiosity, confidence, courage, and consistency, and the greatest of all is confidence. When you believe in a thing, believe in it all the way, implicitly and unquestionably."

The difference between succeeding and failing is the decision you make to persevere or throw in the towel. Do nothing, and the odds of failure increase. Your sales will fall into the abyss. Try, and your chances of success increase tenfold.

As we've said, marketing and promotion are primarily the author's job. For the publisher, it's all about the bottom line. If you aren't selling, they aren't going to take your option book and keep publishing you. The midlist is disappearing.

Let your marketing plan, including your promo materials, work for you. Get people to your website. Encourage them to read excerpts. Whatever you do, don't give up.

 **Toolbox Essential:**

If one of your chapters or writer's groups has a book signing, be sure to see if there is a table to lay out your swag. If there isn't, ask the coordinator if you can set one up. More often than not, you'll be given the green light. All you have to do is ask.

Book Trailers

Book trailers are like commercials for your book. Once again, you can hire a professional to create your trailer, or you can do it yourself. Either way, there are a couple things you want to keep in mind when thinking about doing a book trailer.

- Give little clues to your story that will make the reader want to buy your book. Don't give the entire story away! Think of a book trailer as a blurb of your book, like the back cover.
- Make sure your name, book name, release date, website, and any other websites you own are listed at the end of the trailer.
- Pick music that goes with the theme of your book. You don't want the theme song for *Friday the Thirteenth* if you are making a book trailer for an inspirational.
- Don't steal photos or music that are copyright protected.

A Quickie Book Trailer Tutorial

Tutorial on how to upload a video to youtube: http://www.youtube.com.

Once you have your pictures picked out and saved, start a storyboard on your movie maker program (Movie Maker for a PC, iMovie for your Mac). Import your pictures and play around with the features of your program.

You can also import your music.

Once your pictures are on the time line, you will be able to click on the photo and add text by using the titles and the effects section of the program.

After you have the pictures, music, and text you want, double check your spelling and grammar, then publish your trailer. This will allow you to save your trailer to your hard drive.

That's all there is to it! Granted this was a very simplified tutorial, but you learn by doing.

Put your new book trailer up on Youtube with as many relevant tags as possible. When you are guest blogging, provide the link to the YouTube video, or embed the video with your post by copying the code and providing it to the blog host.

Professional book trailer production companies:

- NoWickiProductions
  www.nowickiproductions.com
- Circle of Seven www.cosproductions.com and RecTV www.readersentertainment.tv

- JKS Communications
  www.jkscommunications.com
- Free websites for your book trailer:
- www.ehow.com—great step by step directions on
  how to make a book trailer
- www.seabreezecomputers.com—provides links
  for free music
- www.incompetech.com—free music

Post book trailers on:
- Book Screening bookscreening.com
- YouTube www.youtube.com
- Book Trailers dot Net www.book-trailers.net
- Your website/blog/grog

"I make a book trailer for all my novels. I
use istock.comand use both free and bought images. You
buy credits on Istock.com, each image is worth different
credits. To keep on the cheaper side, I tend to find photos
under five credits. I use all free music from
incomptech.com. I have a Tonya Kappes youtube
channel,
(http://www.youtube.com/user/tonyakappes?feature=mhe
e). I post the book trailers on my website/blog site, tweet
it, facebook it, and put them in my press kit." ~Tonya

 **Toolbox Essential:**

A book trailer is a great opportunity to provide a visual of your book to readers and get them excited about the upcoming release. Think of your book trailer as the movie trailer. When you hear James Earl Jones do a voiceover, you get excited to see the new movie he's talking about. Same with the book trailer. You need to make it exciting, create anticipation, and longing.

Chapter Eleven: Building a Village

In this chapter:
- Conferences
- Volunteering

Conferences

If you haven't already figured it out, the writing community is really a small world of individuals. While attending the conferences, you will begin to see the same attendees as the last time around. You'll recognize the same names on various listserves you belong to. Listserves are part of email subscriptions you are involved in, such as yahoo or gmail groups. You will start to notice the same names on some of them; these are people who have the same interest in writing and publishing as you do. This means you're building rapport with like-minded people who will continue to be part of your life, even if only in cyber-space.

As we said in Section One, conferences are a great way to build your network with writers and readers. Now that you have a contract and an impending release, conferences hold new potential for you.

Put on your published author glasses and look at things through new lenses. Meet and learn from other authors. Absorb information about the business side of publishing (the stuff you've ignored as you were writing the book of your heart).

Volunteering

And remember to keep volunteering! Just because you're about to be (or are now) published, don't stop building relationships with people. There are thousands of books to buy. Make people want to buy yours by staying involved, showing that you care, and remaining part of the writing community.

Volunteering and attending conferences means you get to rub elbows with other authors. You can also implement the PR buddy system. Remember that old adage: I'll scratch your back if you scratch mine.

Other authors want to be featured on your blog and they want to have your link on their website and vice versa. All you have to do is ask.

Conferences often afford you the opportunity to meet up with booksellers, book buyers, and your agent and/or editor. Sometimes these meetings are formal, scheduled via an appointment. Sometimes they are informal. You can meet up with people at a publisher party, having drinks or dining together.

Be sure to check out next year's conferences and sign up to do book signings or maybe even give a workshop (see Chapter Twelve for more on teaching)—if it fits your PR personality.

Chapter Twelve: Discover Your Inner Teacher

In this chapter:
- Live and Online Workshops

Live and Online Workshops

 "What I've found worked best for me is teaching and giving away free books and writing a lot of books." So says New York Times Best Seller Lori Wilde who teaches at Savvy Authors, Ed2Go, and a variety of other online venues.

We know! You aren't a teacher by trade. You are a writer. But, we also know that you have a ton of knowledge that could help your fellow colleagues.

You are creative, you are a writer, and you can give back. Are you screaming yet? Thinking your PR personality won't allow it? Ready to slam this book closed? Don't do it!

When The Naked Hero grog, when The Naked Hero was founded, there was a collective agreement that we would teach workshops that complimented the theme of the website. We thought readers and writers would want to know why they are drawn to the characters they read and how hard writers work at getting their favorite characters exactly right.

We wanted to take our site, grow the readership, show readers and writers why it's important to strip down the archetypes, and make the whole thing bigger and better than we even imagined.

We dared to dream.

We saw an opportunity and took it.

Being in a grog together allowed us to use our platform to design workshops. This was an easy transition for us since we are both teachers. Our workshops not only promote our website, but also us as writers. Another bonus—we get to network with other authors, readers, and make new friends.

Tonya is definitely in extrovert and loves to do live workshops. At each stage of Tonya's career she develops a workshop to go with it. She is currently traveling to RWA chapters giving her Road To Self Publishing workshop. This is an opportunity to share her knowledge of the publishing path she has taken as well as meeting new writers.

If your PR personality is more introverted, you can put together a workshop with one of your grog partners or another author you have connected with. It's much easier to have a workshop partner than going it alone. It's also much easier to teach online if you're introverted. Once again, no face-to-face contact takes the pressure away.

While we are paid for the workshops we provide, you may start out by doing them gratis. The object isn't to make money off the workshops, but to gain exposure for our books. We have met a lot of aspiring writers and new blog followers.

Melissa teaches a six month long class called Building a Mystery, as well as month long classes, at Savvy Authors: www.savvyauthors.com. She also teaches at a local university in the continuing education department. "Sometimes it's a lot of work, but I always find myself more motivated when I teach. I'm around people who have the same passion I do, and I'm constantly learning, growing as a writer, and honing my craft."

Chapter Thirteen: Community Promotional and Marketing Opportunities

In this chapter:
- Local paper opportunities
- Think outside the Box
- Library opportunity
- Local Book Seller Opportunity
- Radio Interviews
- Book Signings

Local Paper Opportunities

Does your town have a local paper? Do you have a library?

Take a look at your local papers and read the community section. In this section, papers list local news and what better news than a hometown person becoming published.

Melissa's been featured in The Dallas Morning News, as well as in smaller local papers both in Texas and in California. Newspapers are clamoring for a unique angle on an interesting story. Search newspaper websites to find the contact information for features or books. Draft an email pitching yourself as a story, providing the angle they can take to make an article appealing to their audience. Make sure you give newspapers plenty of lead-time, and have your publisher send them an ARC!

If your town has a university, contact their campus newspaper (and radio station) and ask if they'll review your book and/or conduct an interview.

Think Outside the Box

Just as you can host book signings in original venues, search for unique opportunities to promote your book, as well.

> "My family and I have been Revolutionary War re-enactors for more than 10 years. One of my best promotional tools has been to appear for select events in period costume."
> Author Suzanne Adair

Library Opportunities

Libraries are also great ways to get your name out. In April 2011, Melissa was invited to be part of a mystery panel at the Anaheim Public Library's annual fundraising event. They flew her out, put her up at the conference hotel, and sold her books. What great exposure! She's also given talks at several local libraries in the Dallas/Ft. Worth Metroplex. Don't spend too much time away from your writing, but speaking at and supporting libraries is always a good thing.

Most libraries have a local authors section. They will display books and have literature or swag from the author. Their patrons also love bookmarks that are signed by local authors. Go to your local library and look around. Bookmarks are located by the check out or on top of bookshelves for the taking.

Getting to know your local book sellers, big book stores, and independent books stores are great promotional tools. You can ask when they have a spotlight on local authors and local author signings. It gives you the opportunity to leave your name so they can contact you to include you in upcoming signings.

> 66 99 "Over the years we've tried many seat-of-the-pants marketing campaigns, from sending promo surprises for the four weeks leading up to a book's publication (modestly successful), to writing personal letters to favorite stores (much more successful), to personalizing Advanced Reader Copies (highly successful).
>
> I think the most important piece is to try to put a face with the publication—to let the sales force at the store get a sense there's a person behind the book counting on them. They deal with hundreds of books a week, and making yours stand out is difficult if not impossible. But building up good will over the years, keeping a sense of humor and being yourself makes a profound impression in the publishing world, just as it does anywhere." Ridley Pearson, author of more than 22 crime novels for adults and 5 series for young adults.

Radio

"For the last two months, I've been participating in a radio blog. My publisher's publicity team sets up interviews, sends me email confirmations, then on the scheduled dates, I call into the scheduled station or wait to be called. All of this has been a new experience for me, and along the way I've learned a few things. These tips seem simple, but they've helped a lot.

- Have the book I'm discussing in front of me. Sounds like a no-brainer, but I've learned the hard way that it is indeed possible to 'forget' my main characters' names. Being on a live interview can be stressful. In addition, I'm working on a different book now, so the details aren't near as fresh as they used to be.
- Have one or two short, amusing stories ready to tell. This helps everyone become more engaged in your book. Remember, people are listening to the program to be entertained.

Use the time to tell people about future books, too. You might not get another chance to ever 'speak' to this particular audience again, so try to make the best of your ten minutes." Shelley Shepard Gray, www.shelleyshepardgray.com

Radio interviews are becoming more and more popular. National Public Radio has been great at featuring different authors on their many programs, but local stations also like to feature local authors. It's another chance to get your name out into the community.

No matter what your PR personality, we hope you feel comfortable in your own community. Local radio is great for the introvert. It's like hiding behind that computer. Everyone looks great on the radio!

Online radio programs like Blog Talk Radio also provide opportunities for audio interviews Finally, Books on the House (booksonthehouse.com) does Skype Interviews, yet another way to put a voice and face to your name.

Does your local radio station host community shows, like cooking, home design, construction? A station in Tonya's city
hosts a cooking show once a week on a very popular FM station. Once a month there is a book club. The host of the show invited Tonya to participate every month. Tonya jumped at the chance. The host gives Tonya's websites and promotes Tonya as a local writer at the end of each show. It's great free exposure for hundreds of listeners and Tonya only has to give up a couple hours a month.

Lay the groundwork now by developing a list of contacts for local media, including radio, newspaper, and television.

Book Signings, Part One

If book signings are your thing and fit into your PR personality, go for it! It will be up to you to set up the majority of them. Contact your local booksellers, make an appointment to stop by and discuss opportunities to be a presence in the store, and start scheduling.

Don't feel trapped, however. Think outside the box!

What is your book about? Is it set in a yarn shop? Does is have a dog in it? Is it a thriller?

Book stores aren't the only place to do book signings. A friend hosted a book signing for Melissa at her home. She's also been invited to book clubs. Guess what? They love having the author of the book they've just read come to their meeting. And they will have bought your book and will want you to sign it!

Once again, lay the groundwork by setting up book signings now to coincide with the release of your book.

"When I was writing *The Ladybug Jinx*, I started to think about where I'd like to do a release party. Since its set in a floral shop and a friend of mine owns a florist, I had a great idea. Why not do a book signing at her shop? When I emailed her, she immediately got back with me with a resounding yes! It was her florist's 60th anniversary and having a book signing from a local author was a great idea. She actually read in a floral magazine that a lot of florists are doing this with local authors. Viola! A little thinking outside the box turned out to be a great opportunity for me as a local writer, and for her business." ~Tonya

Since Tonya is self-published she didn't go the conventional route, and it worked for her. There is nothing greater than a community embracing their local talent. What an achievement!

"I've found that book signings in venues other than bookstores have been very successful. In bookstores customers will often avoid eye contact with the author, fearing they'll be sucked into a tractor beam and forced to buy a book. At non-bookstore venues an author signing is more of a novelty. People come up to you to chat and more often than not, walk away with a signed book under their arms. I've been extremely pleased with the signings I've done at Curves, for example. The owners are very receptive to the idea and do quite a bit of promo on my behalf ahead of time." Lois Winston, www.loiswinston.com

Section Three: Moving In

When you embarked on your writing journey, you probably started with the mere notion of turning it into a career. Somehow, your thinking shifted and the idea of selling your book became a real possibility. Understanding the role marketing and promotion play in your future is crucial. Sections One and Two in the *Tricked Out Toolbox* have taken you through the basics, from design and laying your marketing and promotion foundation to framing and building a solid structure.

Now your book is in your hands or on your screen. Your name is plastered across the cover. You are no longer an unpublished or soon-to-be-published writer; you are a published author. It's time to shift the way you market yourself, and yes, there are new tools to pack away in your toolbox.

We know you are exhausted. We know it's taken time, energy, and commitment to get here. It's all a juggling game, but don't give up now! You have to dig in and push to get your book noticed.

You are in the home stretch…until your next release.

Chapter Fourteen: Networking, Revisited

In this chapter:
- The PR buddy
- Knowledge is Power
- The Power of Networking, Revisited

> "Never underestimate the power of promoting others. While you help to promote your fellow authors (for example with interviews and contests, guest blog posts, spotlights, re-tweets, etc.) you are also inadvertently establishing your author name. And most authors, I have found, are willing to reciprocate the gesture." Renee Vincent, www.deepintheheartromance.com

The PR Buddy

"I'll scratch your back if you scratch mine." You want the best for your colleagues and they want the best for you. Never is that concept more important than at this point in your career. It's so much easier to have a friend with you on this writing journey, and no matter your PR personality, or your PR Buddy's, you can be there for each other, and you can help each other.

The power of free promotion is invaluable. When you do cross-promotions with your author friends, it's a win situation for both.

You've built a website, blog/grog, and a following. Your author friends (who hopefully bought your book!) also have websites, blogs/grogs, and followers. They probably write in several different genres which broadens the potential audience.

If they post a blog and link back to your site, or have you as a guest blogger, and you do the same—you will both reach potential new readers and book buyers.

The Girlfriend Cyber Circuit, a virtual tour for female authors, is an example of PR Buddies in action. Twelve authors participate in this closed group. When one of them has a new release, they each blog about it on their individual blog sites, helping to build the buzz and spread the word. Melissa Senate, one of the Girlfriend Cyber Circuit participants explains: "What is the Girlfriends Cyber Circuit, you ask? It's a group of varied and diverse female authors (from chick-lit to mystery to literary to romance and more) who blog about each other's must-read new novels."

Start your own cyber circuit!

Tonya along with three other authors decided to do Madness Under The Mistletoe Christmas anthology. This is a PR Buddy move on all sides. Not only will Tonya's readers buy the anthology to read her story, A Superstitious Christmas, but the other authors' readers will also purchase the book. Each authors' readers have now discovered three new writers to follow.

The power of a PR Buddy and cross-promotion is an amazing discovery.

Guest blogging on a PR Buddy's personal blog site leads to some of their readers commenting on your personal blog. They become crossover readers, and that's just what you want.

"Whenever someone comments on my blog, I always send them a personal email letting them know how much I appreciate their time and comment on the blog. I want my readers to know how much I appreciate them and value them." ~Tonya

What Tonya does may seem like a lot of work, but it works for her PR personality and she enjoys reaching out to her public.

Street Teams are another grass roots concept. A Street Team is a group of readers who love your books and will help spread the word. Offer special perks to these super fans as an incentive to proselytize your book. Give them ARC's, swag, run contests just for them, honor them on your site, etc. Begin building your Street Team early in the game and let it grow.

Knowledge is Power

Giving your time and sharing your knowledge of the craft is another way to spread your networking reach after you are published.

Every writers' group is looking for a free, yes, free, way to connect with other writers or readers. Being a published author puts you in a whole new category.

Readers and writers love to pick published authors' brains. They want to know about your journey, the ins and outs of how you got published, what you do to get your name out there, your craft tips, etc. You name it, they want to know.

If talking to a local writers' group fits with your PR personality, then go for it! Contact them; don't wait for them to contact you. If you can offer it for free or minimal cost, that's even better exposure. Not only will they love you for being free, but they will be more willing to put those free dollars into promoting your lecture in the media and/or buying your books.

We have done our fair share of talking to local writing groups. Once again, we see the power of word of mouth. Remember the Fabergé commercial in Chapter Six? Authors who attended our various talks told other author friends in other parts of the country. Pretty soon requests to have us give talks or workshops started to pour in. Now we are paid to travel across the country, share our experiences, and teach our workshops.

We built our reputation through free networking.

The Power of Networking, Revisited

Networking is hard for everyone, but it is crucial in this writing world. Your PR personality will allow you to network in a way that is comfortable to you.

There are several reasons to keep up with your networking efforts. You want to:

- Stay in the loop
- Know about new writing trends
- Learn new perspectives
- Learn about new opportunities
- Meet new authors
- Build buzz
- Keep a positive attitude
- Stay with it
- Have a sounding board with people who understand

Social Networking is important, too. It'll help you:
- Reach out to readers
- Reach out to other writers
- Stay in the writer's world
- Get free exposure
- Gain recognition
- Do quick little bursts of promotion

Add a workshop section to your website detailing what you teach or your areas of expertise. Melissa and Tonya have been contacted by several many writing groups and have spoken at many meetings (both together and separately), all as a result of the workshop information available on their websites and the platforms they've developed. They've also been speakers at a large regional conferences and have been flown out to various parts of the country to participate in library or writing chapter events.

If a door opens, step through it. You never know where it might lead you.

Writer's groups are always looking for guest speakers. Most of the time they pay a small honorarium for your time.

Chapter Fifteen: Building a Sturdy Website

In this chapter:
- Building Your Opt-In Mailing List
- Ways to direct people to your website
- Ethical Bribes or Bartering Strategies
- Balancing Content and Frequency

Building Your Opt-In Mailing List

Having a list of people who want to hear about your news, contests, and latest books is a goal you should strive for. Building your online e-mailing list, then, is one of the most important things you can do. The end goal is to build interest about you and your brand, making people that much more likely to buy your books as they come out.

For starters, we suggest using an opt-in email management company to easily manage your mailing list.

Opt-in email means someone chooses to receive "bulk" email from you in the form of email, a newsletter, or some other advertising. Sending bulk email without permission is considered spam, so permission is required, hence the term opt-in.

From there, the trick is getting people to your website. Every email you send should direct people back to your website via your Sig File, or signature line. The Sig File is also found at the end of article and blogs you write.

" **"** "As helpful as it might be to advertise our books generally, I think we all know how important it is to get word out about our latest projects to those people who are the most interested in our writing. I've made it a priority to build my online mailing list so I can try to connect directly with loyal readers and with people who I know are curious about my stories. About four times per year (once every season), I send out a free e-newsletter. I have a sign-up for it on my blog and website, but I also encourage readers to join in by offering online giveaways for subscribers, hosting contests, and trying to make the newsletter content as fun and as full of reader extras as possible (i.e., with recipes, info on freebies, random drawings for prizes, first looks at new excerpts, etc.). I also believe having an online presence on blogs and social media sites is really helpful—not necessarily for marketing directly, but for getting to know potential readers and giving them a chance to get to know you and your writing style." Marilyn Brant, marilynbrant.com.

Ways to Direct People to Your Website

- If you've done a blog tour (see Chapter Seventeen), run a simultaneous contest on your site which requires people to opt-in on your mailing list
- Use social networking to alert people about giveaways at your website
- If you have books that are published, create an Amazon author page and link back to your website
- On your Facebook fanpage
- Link back to your website and contests in your email signature line
- If you write articles, include information about your mailing list

Ethical Bribes or Bartering Strategies

Once your target audience discovers your website, you need to get them to actually *join* your mailing list by offering them something. Some people call this an "ethical bribe." We call it a good bartering strategy. Basically, you are offering a freebie or something you're willing to give away in return for a person's contact information—their name and email address. (You can use this bartering strategy at book signings, too!)

The Naked Hero website uses password protected content as a bartering strategy. People subscribe to become members of the site, affording them exclusive access to The Naked Notes, which includes writing tips and mini lessons.

Possible Ethical Bribes/Bartering Tools:

- free ebooks
- excerpts or sample chapters
- podcast
- other giveaways
- partner with other businesses to build your list with giveaways
- ezines sent weekly, bi-monthly, or monthly (note: make the ezine content manageable. Too much information is time-prohibitive for most busy people.)

Your website should include an opt-in box in the top left or right of your site. Creating a separate page on your site with your mailing list information is also a good idea.

Balancing Content and Frequency with your Opt-In List

The last things to consider when sending opt-in emails/newsletter to your mailing list are content and frequency. People are inundated with spam and unsolicited emails these days. It's all too easy to click unsubscribe, and you don't want your email message to be the tipping point for your email recipients.

The other fallout from mass emails is that there is a noticeable decline in the number of people actually clicking to open them. The trick is not abusing your mailing list by sending emails too often, and by making your content something people want to read. Be careful not to be overly promotional. Include fun content that engage people into reading.

There are two theories on frequency:
- often, so you stay in the minds of the people on your email list

OR

- too frequently, so people are tempted to unsubscribe

A final note:
We believe in the old adage that less is more. Send your mass emails sparingly, but make them content heavy.

There are many opt-in management companies to use. Here are a few to get you started:

- Aweber: www.aweber.com
- Mail Chimp: www.mailchimp.com
- Results Mail: www.resultsmail.com
- Constant Contact: www.constantcontact.com
- My Newsletter Builder: www.mynewsletterbuilder.com (Tonya and Melissa use this one)

Chapter Sixteen: Marketing

In this chapter:
- Musts for your Press Kit
- Examples of Press Kit Bios
- More Printable Promotional Items
- Advertising
-

Simply put, a press kit contains press material related to your book (see Appendix E). The press kit can be simple or fancy, depending upon your budget and your creativity. The key, as always, is to have written a good book. Your press kit will capture the interest of the media, including radio and television. Gather your contacts, compile your Press Kit, and send it out!

A press kit doesn't consist of a lot of material, but what you do include is key.

Musts for your Press Kit

- Author bio, both short and long versions
- 300 dpi author photo
- Cover flat, if applicable
- Sell sheet
- Cover quotes from well known authors
- Reviews

You should also have an online Press Kit on your website. Don't make readers hunt for your media page.

Make sure your website is easy to navigate with a tab dedicated to your Press Kit.

Your personal and your agent's contact information can be included in your Press Kit, or it can be under a separate tab, your choice. If you don't have an agent and are self-published, make sure your contact information is clearly visible.

Examples of Press Kit Bios

Short Bio:
Melissa Bourbon, who sometimes answers to her Latina-by-marriage name Melissa Ramirez, gave up teaching middle and high school kids in Northern California to write full-time amidst horses and Longhorns in North Texas. She fantasizes about spending summers writing in quaint, cozy locales, has a love/hate relationship with yoga and chocolate, is devoted to her family, and can't believe she's lucky enough to be living the life of her dreams.

Longer Bio:
Melissa Ramirez/Melissa Bourbon is the marketing director for Entangled Publishing. She is the author of the Lola Cruz mystery series: *Living the Vida Lola* (January 2009) and *Hasta la Vista, Lola!* (February 2010) from Thomas Dunne Books/St. Martin's Minotaur, and Bare Naked Loa (April 2012) from Entangled Publishing, and A Dressmaker's Mystery series for NAL: the bestselling *Pleating for Mercy*, August 2011, *A Fitting End*, February 2012, and *Deadly Patterns*, October 2012. Her

two romantic suspense novels, *A Deadly Curse and A Deadly Sacrifice,* will also be published in *2012.*

A former middle and high school teacher, this blonde-haired, green-eyed, proud to be Latina-by-marriage girl loves following Lola and Harlow on their many adventures. Whether it's contemplating belly button piercings, visiting nudist resorts, or hanging out with seamstresses, she's always up for the challenge. Melissa has two middle grade series for girls in development, is published in Woman's World Magazine and Romance Writers Report, and GLOW Magazine (11/2010), and has a children's book published.

She fantasizes about spending summers writing in quaint, cozy locales, has a love/hate relationship with yoga and chocolate, is devoted to her family, and can't believe she's lucky enough to be living the life of her dreams.

(Visit www.trickedouttoolbox.wordpress.com for an online example)

Tonya's Bio:

Tonya Kappes is an International bestselling and Amazon Movers and Shakers author. She writes about quirky characters and even quirkier situations in the genre of women's fiction and cozy mystery. She's also the author of several short stories, and can be found in several anthologies. *Tricked Out Toolbox: Promotional And Marketing Tools Every Writer Needs*, co-authored with Melissa Bourbon is her nonfiction debut.

She's the princess, queen and jester of her domain which includes her BFF husband, her four teenage boys and two dogs.

For Tonya's upcoming releases, latest news, tons of fun, and way cool contests, check out her website at tonyakappes.blogspot.com.

A sell sheet is an important part of your press kit. Use sell sheets to promote your books at bookstores and libraries. It's a flyer with your book covers, ISBN, and blurbs so the target audience you send these to will know exactly what you are about without them having to hunt down your website or Amazon account. You can mail the sell sheet flyers or email them as a PDF. Visit trickedouttoolbox.wordpress.com for specific example of a sell sheet. (Appendix H: Sell Sheet Checklist)

In order to give your printed materials the most bang, make sure you include:

- Your website, email, and other contact information
- Your brand and/or tagline
- More printable promotional items
- Sticky Notes
- Pens
- Posters
- Bookmarks
- Postcards
- Business Cards
- Signs
- Mouse Pads
- T-shirts

A final note about printed promotional materials: They can be very effective, but use them strategically, don't overspend on them, and stick to your marketing plan and budget.

Advertising

Advertising is a big money word, and another toolbox element to think about. The first big question to answer is: Do you have an advertising budget? If the answer is yes, you have the potential to reach people via print ads, as well as online.

For marketing on a dime, you may have to be more frugal. Do you have the budget for a Publisher's Lunch ad ($900+ for a one-time banner)? How about the ducats for a print ad in Romance Writer's Report (the price ranges from $100 for a 1/6 page ad to $1350 for a full color back cover ad) or the $4000 for a center spread in Romantic Times Book Reviews?

If you are published at Amazon, you can check out Kindle Nation. There are several tiers of advertising with different costs. The sponsorship go out to over thousands and thousands of subscribers. This promotion yields strong ROI (return on investment), bumping sales in the short term, and continuing to impact them after the push is over. Other options include sites like Lee Hyat's Author Sound Relations and Leena's Goodie Room, as well as Featured Authors week at Books on the House (http://booksonthehouse.com)

Weigh your options and give careful consideration to which venue will garner the most bang for your buck. Will the money it costs to produce and place a print ad reach more people for a longer period of time if you direct that money toward online banner ads on high traffic sites?

Don't forget about guest blogging. This is free advertising at its best. Check www.alexa.com or another website stat tracking site to target sites with high traffic. Remember to use the PR buddy system, remembering to pay it forward.

A great place to search for blogs that want to review your books or have you guest is Book Blogs (http://bookblogs.ning.com/). Blogs are listed by genre which makes it easier for you to select blogs with your target readership. There are hundreds of participating blogs which are reader and writer centric, many will post a review for you as well.

Unfortunately, the return on advertising, in general, is difficult to quantify. Take care not to overspend on promotion where success is difficult to evaluate.

Chapter Seventeen: Blog Tours and Contests

In this chapter:
- Why Do a Blog Tour?
- The Ins and Outs
- Contests
- Giveaways

Why Do a Blog Tour?

We are in the midst of the digital age which begs the question: How many authors hit the road for a traditional book tour?

The answer? Not very many.

With bookstores closing left and right, the rapid growth of e-books, and the changing economics of the publishing industry, that road trip certainly isn't going to be funded by the publishing house, and it's probably not the best use of your marketing dollars.

So how do you reach a lot of people in the most time and cost efficient way?

The answer? A virtual book tour.

Blog touring is one of the author's most effective ways to promote and market their book and it's also one way to make a great and long-lasting impression on your potential readers.

A virtual or blog tour utilizes the vast resources and community on the World Wide Web, all from the comfort of your home. There are many advantages to virtual/blog tours:

- There is no travel involved! This is especially great if you identified yourself as an introvert in Chapter One. No need to go face-to-face and make conversation with readers, no public speaking, and no pressure.
- Targeted exposure. You can visit blogs with a focus on your genre, making it more likely that you will reach your target audience.
- Guest blogs are the promotions that keep on giving. Unless a blog site is taken off-line, your post is part of the blogosphere for all eternity. It is perpetual marketing.
- Introduction to an audience who might never have found you on their own. Once again, you're building relationships.
- Guest posts are about you and your book. You can also delve into your writing techniques, and other interesting facets of your publishing journey. It's a way to let your personality shine, giving readers a way to connect with you.
- Participating in a blog tour means you're getting concentrated exposure during a short period of time. This is how buzz

starts. The potential for word of mouth exposure is great.

- Spreading your blog tour out over an extended period of time means continued exposure and is an alternate approach to your blog tour structure. It guarantees that your book remains in the consciousness of potential readers for a longer period of time. As long as you promote your book, you will gain sales.

The Ins and Outs

There are two ways to set up a blog tour. Hire a professional virtual tour company, or do it yourself.

As with anything, when you hire someone to do work for you, you free yourself up to spend your time on other things, but the financial investment is greater. Hiring a virtual tour company means someone else will do the legwork of contacting bloggers, setting up your guest posts, delivering the columns you provide to the blog sites, and any other logistics relevant to the tour.

What this means for you is more dedicated time for writing—your first love.

- Pump Up Your Book Promotion
  www.pumpupyourbookpromotion.com

- SORMAG—Shades of Romance Magazine
  www.sormag.com
- Nia Virtual Book Tours
  www.niavirtualbooktours.com
- Bewitching Blog Tours
  www.bewitchingbooktours.blogspot.com
- Author Buzz www.authorbuzz.com
- Author Sound Relations
  www.authorsoundrelations.com

However, if hiring a professional company is not in your budget, go the DIY route. Planning your own blog tour is not as tough as you might think.

- Spend some time searching for blogs that review books, particularly books in your genre. Make a list.
- Contact the site owner with a personal email asking if they would like to host you as a guest. Generally, offering them and/or their readers a complimentary book is considered good form.
- Keep a calendar of all the bookings you get.
- Begin writing the guest posts. Each blog has a personality. Quirky. Formal. Fun. Smart. Sassy. Chatty. Make sure each of your guest posts reflect the tone of each blog.
- Submit your blogs in a timely manner, as well as any review or giveaway copies of

your book. You are a professional. Your host blog owners will appreciate your professionalism.

Whether you go with a professional blog tour or set up your own by contacting websites with high traffic and your targeted audience, there are three things to remember when it comes to blog tours:

- You get out of it what you put into it.
- Giveaways and fresh material are essential.
- Be an active participant.

These seem like basic concepts, but you'd be surprised how many authors put zero effort into the blog tours they've set up and/or are paying for, how few do giveaways or post fresh material (blogs) at each stop of the tour, and most importantly, how few actually show up at the blog site and participate by responding to the comments.

Let's take these elements one at a time. First, like anything else worth your time, if you devote the time and energy, the reward will be greater. If you take the time to create individual blogs which reflect the tone of a blog tour stop, for example, your blog host is more likely to respond favorably to you because you've shown interest in him/her. If you send confirmation and follow up thank you emails, you've acted professionally and have worked at building rapport with the blog host. S/he will be that much more likely to host you next time you have a book come out.

You're building relationships, both with readers and with the blog hosts. Be professional and put a little effort into it. The payoff will be great.

 **Toolbox Essential:**

- Post your blog tour schedule with links on your website. Make it easy for people to follow your tour.

- With each guest post, include links back to your website, Amazon, Barnes & Noble, etc, and your other blog tour stops.

- Make sure you come by each blog you're guesting at and leave comments.

- Send a follow-up Thank You email to the blog owner. Building a good relationship and being gracious means they'll be more inclined to welcome you back the next time around.

- It is typical to give away a book at each stop on your blog tour. Schedule as many stops as you have books to give away.

- Reach out to Fresh Fiction (www.freshfiction.com) and their blogs for maximum exposure.

"

"Be unique with your blog tour. On my recent tour for *Losing Faith*, I reworked interviews and guest posts until they were all different from one another, fun, and informative. I also included deleted scenes and excerpts readers couldn't find elsewhere. Offer readers something for following along your blog tour and make it worthwhile for them. I asked my publisher for books and they supplied me with so many I was able to provide three grand prizes of ten books each! Plus I included iTunes cards to go with the playlist day, poetry journals and T-shirts. If you're going to do a blog tour, my advice is this: plan well in advance. Put a lot of effort into it to make it memorable, and it will be worth it—both for you and the people who follow along." YA author Denise Jaden www.denisejaden.com

Next up are giveaways and fresh material. The point of a blog tour is to GET PEOPLE TO FOLLOW THE TOUR. If you post the same blog or article, or a closely reworked one, the very people you're hoping to attract will become bored. Once again, take the time to deliver fresh and original blogs to each blog host. Your readers want to be entertained. You're a writer. Do your job. Follow up each stop with a giveaway of a free book, or something related to your book. Remember the saying: You have to spend money to make money. It applies to books, as well. You have to give books to sell books. Word of mouth goes a long way.

Third, don't be MIA. Make a point to stop by each website on your blog tour several times each day. Leave comments. Interact with readers. Ask questions. Be engaging. More than that, simply be present.

> "A blog tour can be a fun way to introduce your book to readers. Unfortunately a lot of authors have treated their blog tour like a one day advertisement instead of a book tour." LaShaunda believes that a blog tour takes time and commitment, just like a live book tour does. "If you don't have time, don't do one." LaShaunda C. Hoffman, creator of SORMAG—Shades of Romance Magazine

A virtual/blog book tour can generate buzz about your book. It is a surefire way to reach your target audience. And it can gain you mass exposure with minimal effort. If you're looking for a cost-effective, time-efficient way to find potential readers, a virtual/blog book tour is the way to go.

One final note on blog tours: It's not hard to reach book lovers who frequent book blogs. Often, however, the challenge is bring your book to the masses. How do you reach people outside of the author and book blog world?

Find other online communities where your target audience visits. Offer to guest blog at pet sites, sewing sites, or whatever type of site hooks into a them in your book.

When I was planning my marketing approach for Pleating for Mercy, I decided to target sewing blogs because the series centers around a fashion designer-turned dressmaker. I searched for high traffic sites that appeal to fabric lovers and sewers. I sent out emails offering ARC's of the book and asking for the opportunity to guest blog. The response was phenomenal, and the result was exposure to people outside the typical book blog circuit. I place inexpensive ads on sewing community sites like Sew What's New (http://sew-whats-new.com/). The results of my efforts? Pleating for Mercy hit the Barnes and Noble and Bookscan mass market mystery lists during its first several weeks."~Melissa

Contests

Everyone loves to win!

When we host a contest on our own blogs, we do it because we want to give back to our readers. We aren't saying break the bank with contests. You don't have to give away Kindles, Nooks, Kobos, Sony eReaders, or iPads. A token of thanks is enough to give back to those who've helped make you successful.

What do we give away?

It depends on the time of the year. Gift copying your book is a great way to show appreciation to your readers. Sometimes we will give away coffee packets, mugs, lotions, bath items, books we've picked up free at conferences, hats...you name it—we give it away.

We don't spend a lot of money. Shop sales and dollar stores. We are always perusing the clearance items at stores we frequent. There are some really unbelievable deals out there.

When you mail off a gift to a contest winner, don't forget to throw in some of those promotional items announcing your new book deal! After all, that is what this is all about! We want to sell your book to that winner!

Another reason we hold contests is to hear from our readers. We love our blog and Facebook followers. We want them to know we appreciate them. Going the extra mile to hold a contest is one of the best ways to show that appreciation.

If you don't have books to give away, you can include an IOU. If you or your publisher has Advanced Reading Copies (ARCs), send one of those! If you self-publish, send a PDF file of your novel. If you do send an ARC, ask the contest winner to write a review and post it online at Amazon, Barnes & Noble, Goodreads, etc. The more buzz, the better.

Giveaways

We said it once, but it bears saying again: You have to give away books to sell books. This works especially well if you have backlist e-books or remaindered print books. Let your past sell your future. Your goal is always

 **Toolbox Essential**:

Give away an IOU of your upcoming book or

advance reading copy. Then ask the winner to give

a review. It's a great opportunity for both of you!

to get people interested in your books. What better way to do that than to offer excerpted booklets or copies of your book?

Indie published author, Jennifer Laurens gives away free copies of the first book in her series to every friend on Facebook. She does this for readers only—not fellow authors. "Fellow authors rarely accept the offering whereas readers LOVE it." She also does weekly giveaways on her blog. Yes, you read right, weekly! It takes time to orchestrate, and regular trips to the post office, but she finds it worth the effort.

"I have 'surprise' freebies I give away to all Twitter followers." Jennifer Laurens, www.jenniferlaurens.com, www.heavenlythebook.com.

She believes giveaways work. We agree. Giveaways, if done with regularity, work.

Author Nancy Kay has an extras section on her website where she offers a free holiday story as an enticement. "Although social networks are great for reaching the masses, I think it's important to 'hook', if you will, in a more personal way. To stand out from the gazillion contacts we're inundated with on a regular basis."

Chapter Eighteen: Book Signings, Part Two

In this Chapter:
- More About Book Signings
- Book Signing Tips for your Toolbox

More about Book Signings

"Never underestimate the power of the excerpt (booklet). Online e-newsletters with an exclusive excerpt from your novel are a great way to entice the reader. Give them a peek at your story, let them get a taste of the tone and the characters in a riveting scene and you'll have them hooked. Chances are strong that next time they're in the bookstore, they'll look for your book.

You don't have time to do a regular newsletter, there are several opportunities available on the internet where you can purchase a one-time e-newsletter slot and get the word out to a very large potential audience. If your budget allows for a true 'mailing', get some flyers or rack cards printed with an excerpt on one side and get them physically in the hands of your readers. In my experience, excerpts are one of the 'best' tools an author can use to

help get those sales numbers up!" Leena
Hyat,

If you are an introvert, right now is a great time to go to book stores and sign stock of your book. Local book stores love authors to come by and sign stock. You can even leave bookmarks or postcards in the books or on the counter by the register for those potential readers who didn't see your book on the shelf. (Turn your books face out on the shelves while you're there, but shhhh, don't be too obvious about it!)

For the extroverts, book signings are a great way to connect with readers who follow you and readers who just happen to be in the store. At book signings be sure to hand out some of the marketing material for the book you are signing and upcoming books.

Don't sit behind a table at a book signing, if you can avoid it. Stand, smile, walk around, hand out your printed materials, and engage people in conversation. It's tough at first, but tuck away your nerves and try to channel the extrovert inside you.

"I always take my book signing notebook with me to all my signings. I use the same notebook until it's filled up with the contact information of readers who stopped by to talk to me at my signings. They might not buy a book that day, but they do leave their name, email address, and physical address in my book. This gives me permission to add them to my email list, newsletter, etc. I even take pictures to add to my website or blog and drop them a note saying I've put them on my site.

Once I get home from a signing, I personally send each person who signed the notebook a free on-line greeting card to thank them for coming." ~Tonya

Again, Tonya reaches out to her readers because she values the time it took them to come to her signing. It builds a great rapport between her and her followers.

Book Signing Tips for Your Toolbox

Your first book signing can be daunting. Do you stand or sit? Engage people or let them come to you? Have goodies or not? Once you understand your PR Personality, you should be able to answer these questions a little better. You have to do what feels comfortable to you, but we have some tried and true tips to help you, whether you're an introvert or an extrovert.

One caveat: don't do them all! Think about each one and determine what will work for you. Each store is different. Work with the personality of the store hosting your signing.

Also, keep in mind, a book signing is not necessarily about selling books (though that's always desirable). It's about building relationships with booksellers (hand selling by these book experts is KEY!) and with potential readers. They many not buy your book at the signing, but may well pick it up next time they're in the store, or search for it at a later date.

As always, learn, grow, and develop your marketing and promotion strategies as you figure out what works for you and what doesn't.

Before the Book Signing:

Tip # 1: Make enlargements of your book cover at a local copy shop. You can have the shop laminate the poster and put them on a poster board. Alternatively, you can purchase spray-on adhesive, buy your own poster board, and attach the poster yourself.

Tip #2: Make a "Book Signing Kit"
- Several pens. Thin tipped Sharpies work well, or any pen that writes well and won't bleed.
- A notepad to write down the spelling of people's names.
- A notebook or Mailing List signup sheet.
- Sticky notes to help patrons identify books you've signed for multiple people.
- Bookmarks, postcards, and other print material to include with each book.
- Signed by author or Autographed Copy stickers.

Tip #3: Ask the bookstore if they have media resources/media kit they can provide you (for TV, radio, etc) which provides information on local media they've used or have contacts with. If they do, it will save you the legwork of hunting down contacts.

Tip #4: Once you have this information, call them! Time the call to within about a month of your signing. Invite them to the event. Tell them about your signing and book and request an interview. Offer to send them an ARC of your book, as well.

Tip #5: Send a press announcement to the local newspaper(s) about your signing. The bookstore may do this, as well, but best to take matters into your own hands. Remember, newspapers need a lead time of at least a week, sometimes longer. Plan accordingly.

Tip #6: Contact the local paper and suggest they do a feature article on you. Tell them you are available to be photographed at the book signing if something can't be arranged earlier.

Tip #7: Send evites, print invitations, send out postcards, call friends and family to announce your book signing. Let your local writing chapter members know, as well.

Tip #8: Make a printable sheet of your book reviews to set out at the signing table. You can hand these to people who stop and express interest in your book.

Tip #9: Prepare to stay longer than the allotted time for the signing. You often sell more books, make more contacts, and build rapport with the booksellers after the event is officially over!

The Day of the Signing:

Tip #1: Show up early. You want time to be shown the table or area where you will sign or give your talk, give an overview of your book to the store personnel, set up your materials, and take a deep breath.

Tip #2: Take a few minutes to introduce yourself to store personnel and give them an overview of your book. Also, ask to have a stack of your books displayed at the register. They redirect interested patrons back to you!

Tip #3: At the store, turn your books face out on the shelves!

Tip #4: Ask if a staff member will read an announcement about your signing. Come prepared with a brief statement written on a card for someone to read from. Ask them to repeat the announcement every half hour.

Tip #5: Greet customers! Be friendly! Smile! Walk around with your book! Shake hands!

Tip #6: Don't just sit behind a table if you can avoid it. Many people think authors are unapproachable. If you're standing up and smiling, you will dispel this myth, at least about yourself.

Tip #7: Hand people your book. Most people will take something handed to them, and then take another moment to look at the front, back, and flip through the pages.

Tip #8: After you've introduced yourself and engaged in a brief conversation, be quiet! Give the person looking at your book a few moments of silence so they can actually read the back blurbs, cover flap, or first page.

Tip #9: Pass out bookmarks, postcards, other printed materials and swag you have. For example, Tonya made fun Mardi Gras type masks to give out at her signing for *Something Spooky This Way Comes*, featuring her story, "Masked Souls."

Tip #10: Bring a PR Buddy to help pimp your books! It's often easier for someone else to engage strangers in conversation about your book. You'll have a chance to return the favor at your friend's book signing. (A friend or family member can do this, too.)

Tip #11: Have someone take pictures of you signing books, as well as with the store manager, customer relations manager (CRM), and other store personnel. Be holding your book, or have a book display in the background! Put them up on your website! Get their email address and send the picture to your reader. Mail a copy (framed and signed) to the store and/or manager.

Tip #12: Have someone take pictures of you and the people who buy your books. Use a Polaroid camera, if you can, or use a digital camera and offer to email the new reader the picture.

Tip #13: Have sweet treats to give away. Everyone loves candy! If you create a tie-in to your book, all the better, but individually wrapped chocolates are always a hit. These encourage people to stop at the table. They also keep kids busy while parents look at your book.

Tip #14: Pass out FREE raffle tickets and raffle off a small prize. Have customers put their names and email addresses on the back of the ticket. Now they have a chance to win whatever you're giving away (a gift card to the book store you're signing at is always a good choice. So are gift baskets, or other items which tie into your book) and you have collected additional email addresses for your mailing list. Raffle something off each half hour and have the winner announced over the store's loud speaker for maximum effect.

Tip #15: Bring in visuals that relate to your book. For example, Melissa will use a decorative dress form on the signing table when promoting *A Magical Dressmaking Mystery Series*.

Tip #16: Before you leave, ask to sign stock. Most stores love to have signed copies of an author's books.

Tip #17: Ask that the store place your book in the 'recommended' section and/or local authors section for maximum exposure. Don't be afraid to ask for anything! The worst they can say is no, but if you never ask, it's a guaranteed no.

Tip #18: Bring a small token gift to the store manager or whoever set up your signing, if you feel it's appropriate. A $5 coffee card or a small box of chocolates will do the trick. Don't give one of your promotional items!

Tip #19: After your book signing event, send a thank you note to the personnel, store manager, CRM, or whoever organized the book signing.

"I'm self-published and I have print on demand through Createspace. I've always wanted to participate in book signings. My local book store allows me to bring my own books to different events. I also bring my laptop just in case a readers wants to buy a digital version of one of my books right then and there. I'm also on Kindlegraph (www.kindlegraph.com) with over 3k other authors. Readers can request the autograph of any author, who has an ebook. It's a pretty cool tool for your toolbox. Check it out! Book signings are for everyone, no matter what your publication path is. Another one of my author friends and Carina press author, Keri Stevens, her books are only ebooks. She too takes a laptop to book signings so readers can buy her novel, Stoned Kissed. She also wears a t-shirt with a QR Code that links a smart phone straight to her Amazon buy link. In the restaurant she had four people buy her book just because her shirt was so cool!" ~Tonya

QR codes are a fantastic tool. Essentially, they are scannable 2D barcodes which link to the landing page of your choice (QR scan apps are available to download for any smart phone).

The goal of using a QR code is getting people to take immediate action. You want a quick response. Don't link to your homepage or Facebook account. There's nothing to motivate a potential reader to stay there. Offer something actionable through your QR code. Link the code to an excerpt and a free download of your newest release. Or go straight for the jugular and connect the QR code to the buy link of your book.

Shorten your link using bitly.com or tinyurl.com.

Finally, be creative in how you incorporate a QR code into a promo item. Embed it into a visual/graphic design, or come up with a clever slogan. Then put it on your business cards, postcards, bookmarks, t-shirts, or totes (for starters).

Entangled Publishing sponsored the North Texas RWA chapter's Texas Two-Step conference by providing tote bags to attendees with our Lori Wilde's Indulgence category line logo. I incorporated a QR code into the design so attendees could download a free Indulgence book. Using the QR code offered an immediate way for our target audience to try our product, thus we were able to begin building brand loyalty and reader expectation." ~Melissa

Generate QR Codes at these, and other, sites:

- http://qrcode.kaywa.com/
- http://www.qrstuff.com/
- http://www.qurify.com/en/
- http://delivr.com/qr-code-generator
- http://goqr.me/

Chapter Nineteen: Settling In

In this Chapter:
- Filling Up Your Toolbox

Filling Up Your Toolbox

Your toolbox is ever-changing. As you discover what works for you, and what doesn't, you will pare down, reorganize, gather more materials, and truly make it your own. The *Tricked Out Toolbox* is not a magic bullet to the New York Times best sellers list or six-figure book deals; it is a compilation of practical marketing and promotional tools we've found to be useful in our careers.

Filling your toolbox should be an easier task thanks to the valuable insight from industry professionals and other authors who've tested the water for you, but the bottom line is that there is no tried and true method to success. If you do nothing, nothing will be the result. Take action and be the builder of your own career.

It's up to you to decide what to put in your toolbox.

Become a member of the *Tricked Out Toolbox* website and gain access to our exclusive pintables based on the appendices in this book, as well as articles on marketing and promotion. URL: trickedouttoolbox.wordpress.com

Your member password for the site is: trickedout

See you there!

Tonya and Melissa

Appendix A: Your Killer Marketing Plan: Decisions, Decisions, Decisions!

Use this worksheet to help identify the best marketing tools based on your PR personality. (Remember these can be downloaded from the *Tricked Out Toolbox* Website (http://trickedouttoolbox.wordpress.com/).

Marketing Tool: _____ _____ (Website, post cards, book marks, etc.)	Notes:
Goal: _____ _____ (Be specific: what do you want to achieve with this particular marketing tool?)	Notes:
Cost: _____ _____ (Be very specific: design, production, shipping, postage.)	Notes:
Budget: _____ _____ (Refer to your budget	Notes:

worksheet and how this particular marketing tool fits.)	
Time: _____ _____ (How much of your time is this going to require and do you have that time—from design to completion.)	Notes:
Target Date: _____ _____ (When do you want to have it done? Do you have enough time and will it be useful?)	Notes:
Inconvenience: 1 2 3 4 5 6 7 8 9 10 (How much hassle is this going to be for you? Are you dreading it=1 Or excited=10? Is the effort worth the payoff?)	Notes:

Impact: _____ _____ _____ (How is this tool	Short-term	Long-term

going to impact your goal?)			
Outcome: ___ ___ ___ __ (Decision of whether or not you are going to use the tool.)	No	Maybe	Yes
Notes:			

Appendix B: Action Plan Checklist

Take this checklist and use it to fill in your Action Plan Timeframe Worksheet

- ❑ Set up your own blog/website
- ❑ Begin contacting the people on your list to set up a blog tour to gain exposure (or contact a professional blog tour company like Pump Up Your Book Promotion)
- ❑ Make a list of websites to contact for guest blogging
- ❑ Make a list of online review sites
- ❑ Prepare or/and create postcards, bookmarks, ARCs, etc and send to reviewers. (Make sure the sites get a lot of traffic.)
- ❑ Set up local signings
- ❑ Do targeted mailings of a post card to friends, family, independent bookstores, etc.
- ❑ Identify potential radio venues
- ❑ Contact radio stations to try to set up interviews
- ❑ Create a Press Kit (see Chapter Sixteen)
- ❑ Send out your press kit

Appendix C: Laying out Your Action Plan Timeframe

Timeframe	Goal/Objective	Action
Six Months Out		
Five Months Out		

Timeframe	Goal/Objective	Action
Four Months Out		
Three Months Out		

The Tricked-Out Toolbox

Timeframe	Goal/Objective	Action
Two Months Out		
One Month Out		

Timeframe	Goal/Objective	Action

Appendix D: Goal Setting/Dare to Dream Worksheet

Setting attainable goals is the foundation of success. If your goals aren't attainable, you're setting yourself up for failure. Use this worksheet to identify attainable goals.

What do you Dare to Dream? Now is the time to be very honest with yourself. Are you writing for yourself or to be published? Do you want to be a NY Times Bestseller? Whatever this dream is, it may feel light years away, but don't worry about that now. Identifying it (or them) will help you stay the course.	

Where do you see yourself in five years? Think about what you dared to dream. Did you reach for the stars? If you want to be on the NY Times Bestseller list, is that with your first book? Subsequent books? In five years, will you have already attained bestsellerdom, or will you be paving the way? Or maybe you want to write the Great American Novel. Is a Master of Fine Arts Degree in your future?	

Transforming Dreams into Action Successful marketing depends upon the end goal (s). What do you need to do now, a month from now, a year from now, etc., to reach the dreams you've dared to dream? If you want to write a book a year and hit the NY Times list by the third book, exposure is key. You can write the best book in the world, but if people don't know it's out there, you'll never hit that list. Think about everything you've read in the *Tricked Out Toolbox* and identify what you can do to help you reach your dreams.	

Appendix E: Press Kit Checklist

You can get creative with your physical press kit (example: package it in a Chinese take-out box if your book has Chinese themes/food).

The simple approach is to buy a three-ring binder and create a book cover replica to paste on the front. Inside, include the following items, staggered or tiered within the flaps and boldly titled for an easy at-a-glance perusal. Check out trickedouttoolbox.wordpress.com for example photos.

- ❏ Author bio, both short and long versions
- ❏ 300 dpi author photo
- ❏ Cover flat, if applicable
- ❏ Sell sheet
- ❏ Cover quotes from well known authors
- ❏ Reviews

Appendix F: Marketing Budget Worksheet

Item	Budgeted	Actual	Difference
Postage: ARCs, postcards, bookmarks, press kits, etc.			
Production Costs: bookmarks, postcards, etc.			
Advertising: Books on the House (booksontheh ouse.com), AuthorBuzz, website banners, etc.			
Website and/or blog construction			

Item	Budgeted	Actual	Difference
Press Kit Materials: flyers, copies of reviews, etc.			
Author photo			
Other swag for book signings and giveaways			
Print ads			
Travel expenses for book signings			
Release party			
NOTES:			

Appendix G: Create a Memorable Tagline

1. A memorable tagline takes a little time and energy.
2. Brainstorm words that represent what you write, emotions you hope to evoke, and your style of writing.
3. Take a good look at your list. Circle the ones that speak to you. Reject the ones that don't seem to fit.
4. Now be creative! Play around with the words, group them together, and see what combinations you can come up with that represent you and your writing.
5. Short is good. Don't worry about making it too zippy—simple is usually better.

Notes:

Appendix H: Sell Sheet Checklist

You can make your sell sheet simple or fancy. Take care not to make it too busy or it risks being unreadable. Include:

- ❏ Author photo
- ❏ Author bio
- ❏ ISBN #s (or ASiN #s)
- ❏ Publisher
- ❏ Book cover(s)
- ❏ Contact info/website URL
- ❏ Reviews

Examples are available at trickedouttoolbox.wordpress.com.

Appendix I: Quick Guide: Implementing Your Marketing Plan after the Call

You've gotten the call, are gearing up for the next phase of your career, but now what? While every publishing house has their own specific procedures, you can expect the following things to happen:

1. Contract Negotiation: This takes place between your agent and editor. Many items are non-negotiable, but your agent will do his/her best to get you the best deal, including your advance and payout schedule.

2. Preparation of Contract: Your publisher prepares your contract, sends to your agent for review and changes. This continues until all terms are agreed upon (often these negotiations happen over the phone). You sign the final copies and return to your agent.

3. Payout: Your payment schedule is negotiated in your contract. Typically, an advance is paid out over three installments. The first payout usually takes place upon signing, which means after the contract has been processed. This can take a while! Other payouts usually happen upon delivery and acceptance of manuscript and again upon publication.

   • Now is the time to begin implementing your marketing plan!

4. Publisher's Plan: You should hear from your editor after you've signed the contract or your deal is accepted. Expect to discuss the timeline for delivery of your manuscript, publisher expectations, pennames, and general marketing plans from the publishing house. As your publication date grows closer, you will probably work with a house publicist.
    - Now is when you should evaluate your website, consider redesigning, tweaking, or enhancing it to reflect your newly contracted book and the brand you've developed.
5. Brainstorming: It's not just for the writing process. Think outside the box for cross-promotional opportunities, authors who might blurb your book (provide a cover quote), and other creative ways to gain exposure for your book.
    - Meanwhile, keep working on the next book in your contract or your next project. As they say, you're only as good as your next book. You can never rest on your laurels.
6. Editorial Letter: Unless you're a rarity, you'll receive an editorial letter from your editor, as well as a deadline to submit your revisions.
    - While working on revisions, continue implementing working on your website, joining Listserves and online groups to build your reputation, and begin thinking about swag or other promotional items.

7. Publisher Questionnaire: Fill out the publisher questionnaire detailing your background, affiliations, marketing ideas, names of people to receive ARCs, etc. Be as detailed as possible. The more information your publicist has to work with, the better.

8. Copy Edits: Your copy editor is your friend! Each publishing house has specific and unique guidelines. The copy editor will read your manuscript with a fine tooth comb and look for grammar, conventions, consistency, repetitive phrasing, awkward sentence structure, etc. You will go through the manuscript and address each concern.

   • Meanwhile, you should be thinking about setting up a blog tour, contacting potential websites, and creating bookmarks or postcards, etc.

9. Galleys: This is the typeset or formatted version of your manuscript. Any changes you make at this point may end up costing you money because new typesetting might be required. This is your final look-through before your manuscript becomes a book.

10. Cover Art: You've probably already seen cover art or art samples. If the art department has provided you with a final version and you have permission, begin sharing your cover to build buzz and garner exposure.

11. The Home Stretch: You should have more contact with your house publicist at this point, finalizing who will be receiving ARCs of your book, as well

as other plans you've made with the publishing house.

- Contact your local bookseller and begin planning your release party. Include friends and media on your guest list. Begin growing your mailing list.

12. ARCs: Your contract will have specified how many ARCs (Advance Reading Copies) you will receive. These are for you to distribute to reviewers, bloggers, etc. Sending out ARCs is your last big pre-publication marketing push.

13. Cover Flats: If you're being published in trade or mass market paperback, you'll receive cover flats of your book cover for distribution at book signings, etc. At this time, send out press kits and include your cover flat (see Chapter Sixteen Press Kit).

- If you're published in hardcover, you may request one or two book jackets, not enough to distribute, however.
- Finalize plans for your release party.

14. Move Forward: Don't let your creativity stall because you're suddenly wrapped up in the business side of publishing. Keep working on your next book or project. Keep blogging. Keep thinking of ways to gain exposure for your book. Soon you'll get copies of your book (as negotiated for in your contract).

15. Enjoy the moment and celebrate!

Appendix J: Website Checklist

Before you start:
- ❏ Know your audience
- ❏ Create a brand
- ❏ Offer fresh content
- ❏ Make navigation simple
- ❏ Have a professional look

Include:
- ❏ Author's bio
- ❏ Excerpt of writing
- ❏ Contact information
- ❏ Press kit
- ❏ FAQ about you as relevant to your writing career, things readers might like to know, etc.
- ❏ Current information on your books
- ❏ Links to articles you've written
- ❏ Workshops
- ❏ Opt-in mailing list

tonya kappes & melissa bourbon ramirez

Appendix K: From Acquisition to Bookstore

Your agent has submitted your manuscript to interested editors. One of them calls with an offer. You reach an agreement and sign a contract. Here's a rundown on what happens after acquisition.

- A publication date is set.
- You will work with your editor on the submission and editing of your manuscript.
- Publisher meeting: your editor will meet with key people regarding your book—sales, marketing, publicity, art.
- Your book is on the docket; meetings in-house will continue to make sure all is on-track.
- The sales person assigned to your book will begin reaching out to bookstore chains. Sales meeting will also take place during this time.
- Copy edits are completed.
- Print run is finalized.
- Galleys are sent out for cover blurbs, magazines with long lead times, and key book reviewers.
- ARCs sent to other reviewers.
- Hopefully, reviews begin to come in from Publisher's Weekly, Library Journal, Booklist, etc.

The Tricked-Out Toolbox

- Book hits the streets.
- The in-store date is when your book is supposed to be in bookstores, ready to sell.

About the Authors

Fiction authors Tonya Kappes and Melissa Bourbon (aka Misa Ramirez) believe that targeted and smart promotion and marketing can take a book from lackluster sales to the world of bestseller. They pooled their resources and knowledge to write *The Tricked Out Toolbox: Promotion and Marketing Tools Every Writer Needs*. When not touting marketing and promotion through their workshops, they write cozy mysteries, romantic suspense, and women's fiction. You can visit their websites at: Tonyakappes.blogspot.com
Misaramirez.com